Sex, Drugs, and Violence in the Jewish Tradition

Sex, Drugs, and Violence in the Jewish Tradition

Moral Perspectives

DANIEL B. KOHN

JASON ARONSON

Lanham • Boulder • New York • Toronto • Oxford

Published in the United States of America
by Jason Aronson
An imprint of Rowman & Littlefield Publishers, Inc.

A wholly owned subsidiary of
The Rowman & Littlefield Publishing Group, Inc.
4501 Forbes Boulevard, Suite 200, Lanham, Maryland 20706
www.rowmanlittlefield.com

PO Box 317
Oxford
OX2 9RU, UK

British Library Cataloguing in Publication Information Available

Library of Congress Cataloging-in-Publication Data

Kohn, Daniel B., 1963–
Sex, drugs, and violence in the Jewish Tradition: Moral perspectives / Daniel B. Kohn
p. cm.
Includes index.
ISBN 0-7657-6180-7 (alk. paper)—ISBN 0-7657-0013-1 (pbk.: alk. paper)
1. Violence—Religious aspects—Judaism. 2. Drugs—Religious aspects—Judaism. 3. Sex—Religious aspects—Judaism.

BM538.P3 K65 2004
296.3'6—dc21 00-061065

Printed in the United States of America

The paper used in this publication meets the minimum requirements of American National Standard for Information Sciences—Permanence of Paper for Printed Library Materials, ANSI/NISO Z39.48-1992.

For Devorah,
my love and partner in life

Contents

Part II: Drugs (Alcohol) in the Jewish Tradition

Part III: Sex in the Jewish Tradition

Introduction

We all have values—whether or not we can articulate them—and many of us also have particularly strong opinions about values. Our values come from our families, our peers, and from our culture. Yet, many people today decry what they perceive as a lack of values being taught, communicated, or acted upon in society. Whether or not this is true, I believe that it is vitally important in every age and every society—wherever Jews may live—to spark discussion and debate about moral conduct relevant to our times.

I believe that we must discuss the most troubling, confusing, and misunderstood areas of human behavior in American society today: namely, dealing with anger and violence, alcohol and drug use, and the sexual behavior of singles and adults of all ages.

Several years ago, I created and taught a class in a private Jewish high school about controversial issues such as smoking tobacco, drinking alcohol, using illegal drugs, dealing with anger, confronting rumors and malicious gossip, masturbation, oral sex, abortion, birth control, and serial monogamy. The discussions, questions, and answers that this class elicited were inspiring and profound. Yet most surprising was that my students were amazed to learn that the Jewish tradition had anything to say about these subjects.

The Jewish tradition does address these sensitive issues and has much wisdom to offer on these both ancient and modern topics. However, be forewarned that this book does not provide any clear cut answers to such difficult questions as "Is it okay to get drunk?" or "Is it appropriate to masturbate?" This book also does not try to persuade anyone to discard their own values and adopt new ones. Instead, it provides resources for reflection and consideration to enable everyone to reach their own conclusions.

When I was a college student, my professor taught the class about the origins of the Democratic and Republican parties and the nature of the American political system. On occasion, she might have inadvertently revealed her own political values, but that was by no means her goal. She simply wanted us to become better informed citizens and participants in our democratic republic.

Similarly, I want to share provocative texts and stories from the Jewish tradition about controversial subjects. If I unintentionally reveal my own moral or ethical standpoint, I apologize, for my goal is to create better educated Jews who will be participants in our general society. I do not believe it is my job as a rabbi, educator, or author to tell anyone else what they ought to believe or how they should behave—that is everyone's individual responsibility. Rather, my role is to provide the sources to help others make informed decisions about their own moral behavior. I want to encourage reflection, discussion, and debate, not stifle it. The more familiar we are with our religious heritage, the better prepared we will be to make difficult moral choices in life.

The Jewish tradition has much wisdom and guidance to offer about the subjects of sex, drugs, and violence. Therefore, we should avail ourselves of these resources within the Jewish religious tradition. This book provides original biblical and rabbinic sources, plus in-depth analysis of these ideas, presented for further consideration, reflection, and discussion. The sources are provided in English translation. While many of the translations are based on the Jewish Publication Society's *Tanakh* and the Soncino Talmud, I have substantially emended them to better reflect the Hebrew text and to enhance their readability. Despite the order of the main topics in the title, I present them in reverse order not only to stimulate and maintain the reader's interest, but also because there is an integral logic of progression and development with violence, through alcohol, to sexuality.

This book is a guide for Jews who want to derive moral and ethical guidance from their religious tradition. The Jewish tradition, however, is not monolithic.

Because there is no central authority in Judaism, every rabbi, sage, and scholar has been free to promulgate their own decisions and interpretations of Jewish law and to publish whatever book they have chosen to write over the last 3,000 years. Given this rich diversity, I have chosen texts and interpretations that represent a fairly normative expression of what have been considered historically legitimate expressions of Jewish values. As with any spiritual tradition, the texts presented are open to individual interpretation and debate. It is not my intention to resolve any debates. Rather, my intention is to elevate them to a higher level of moral discourse and holiness.

Rabbinic sources states that whoever quotes Jewish wisdom and honestly acknowledges the original teacher every-so-slightly hastens the coming of the Mashiah (messiah). Therefore, I especially want to acknowledge the profound influence of Rabbi Michael Gold on my understanding of biblical and rabbinic sources when it comes to the realm of human sexuality. In his book, *Does God Belong in the Bedroom?* (Jewish Publication Society, 1992), Rabbi Gold presented traditional Jewish texts about sex with such clarity, insight, and resounding authenticity, that his analyses have formed the foundation of my own. For a fuller treatment of the topics in this section, I recommend readers to Rabbi Gold's book devoted entirely to this subject.

PART I

Violence in the Jewish Tradition

1

Confronting Gossip

People love to talk. Human beings are social creatures who rely on verbal communication to express the majority of our ideas and feelings to others. We especially love to talk about other people. Some anthropologists even suggest that when human beings developed the capacity to speak, our first words were gossip. They claim that as the population of tribes and villages grew, gossip provided the social glue that bonded large communities together, bringing everyone a sense of connection and solidarity with everyone else. Knowing the intimate, and often inappropriate, details of other peoples' lives helped ensure the survival of our species as we developed larger social groups. If this is true, it is no wonder that gossip is so pervasive in every culture on the planet.

However, gossip also has a negative side. It may be fun to share, but it is often hurtful and even malicious. In the Jewish tradition, gossip is called *Lashon HaRah.*

This literally means "evil tongue" and is the generic term used to describe inappropriate and disparaging speech about other people.

The Hebrew Bible, especially the Torah (the Five Books of Moses), is very concerned with appropriate speech and lists quite a number of specific prohibitions regarding slanderous language:

"Do not go about as a talebearer among your countrymen." [This is the prohibition of being a gossip-monger, in other words, of spreading stories about other people, whether true or false.]

(Leviticus 19:16)

"You must not carry a false rumor; you shall not join hands with the guilty to act as a malicious witness." [This is the prohibition of knowingly spreading false rumors about people.]

(Exodus 23:1)

"You shall not profane My holy name, that I may be sanctified in the midst of the Israelite people—I the Lord who sanctify you." [This is the prohibition of blasphemy; that is, one should not use God's name inappropriately. This verse also shows the sacredness of language in general.]

(Leviticus 22:32)

"You shall not take vengeance or bear a grudge against your countrymen." [This is self-explanatory but can refer to literal or verbal violence. We will explore this further on.]

(Leviticus 19:18)

"A single witness may not validate against a person any guilt or blame for any offense that may be committed . . ." [This deals with the ineligibility of a single witness's testimony to be accepted in a court of law. If the testimony of a single witness is not accepted in court, then certainly a negative report by a single person should not be socially acceptable.]

(Deuteronomy 19:15)

"You shall neither side with the multitude to do wrong . . ." [Although the verse goes on to speak about not giving false testimony, this first part articulates the prohibition of following a majority to commit evil. In other words, one cannot indulge in negative, malicious talk just because others are doing it.]

(Exodus 23:2)

"You shall not insult the deaf . . ." [If one cannot curse someone who cannot hear him, he should certainly not be allowed to curse those who can hear!]

(Leviticus 19:14)

While it is valuable to read and consider the biblical passages from the Torah above, it is important to understand that Judaism today is not the religion described in the Hebrew Bible. Modern Judaism is based on the Bible, but the Jewish religion as it is practiced today throughout the world is not biblical Judaism. Judaism today is Rabbinic Judaism; that is, it is the religion of the first rabbis. Rabbis, with a capital "R," indicates these first generations of Jewish spiritual leaders, who lived nearly two thousand years ago. The Rabbis were the first ones to interpret and update the Torah so that it would make sense to the Jews of their generation.

The Torah consistently emphasizes that the Israelites must sacrifice animals at the Temple in Jerusalem as the primary means to interact with God. However, the following rabbinic text clearly shows how the Rabbis of the Talmud updated the Torah:

> Rabban Yochanon ben Zakkai was once walking with his disciple Rabbi Yehoshua near Jerusalem after the destruction of the Temple [by the Romans in 70 C.E.]. Rabbi Yehoshua looked at the Temple ruins and said, "Alas for us! The place which atoned for the sins of the people Israel through the ritual of animal sacrifice lies in ruins!" Then Rabban Yochanon ben Zakkai spoke to him these words of comfort, "Do not be sad, my son. There is another way of gaining atonement. And what is this other way? We must now gain atonement through deeds of loving kindness." For it is written, "Loving kindness I desire, not sacrifice." (Hosea 6:6) [*Avot D'Rabbi Natan* 11a]

The Judaism that these rabbis created was passed down in oral form for centuries, but eventually it came to be written down and preserved in the classical rabbinic works such as the Mishnah and the Gemara, also known as the Talmud, and the various books of Midrash. These rabbinic works set forth the basic blueprint for Rabbinic Judaism, which is the beginning of modern Judaism as we know it today. Later generations of rabbis followed the examples of these first generations of rabbis, and continued to reinterpret and update the Jewish tradition so that it would make sense and be meaningful in every generation.

The Torah is the source of all Jewish values and rituals. However, to understand the growth and development of modern Judaism, it is crucial to study the classic rabbinic works in order to see how the Rabbis interpreted the Torah. The following passage provides an excellent example of the morality of the Rabbis and how they thought of *Lashon HaRah*:

> Rabbi Alexandri was once calling out, "Who wants life? Who wants life?" All the people came and gathered round him saying, "Give us life!" He then quoted to them, "Who is the man who desires life, loves his days that he may see good in them? Guard your tongue from evil and your lips from speaking guile. Depart from evil and do good, seek peace and pursue it!" (Psalms 34:13–14) [Tractate *Avodah Zarah* 19b]

Although not exactly a magic potion to prolong a person's life, the Rabbis clearly agreed with the philosophy expressed in this Psalm. Controlling what we say is a biblical prescription for living a good and long life. However, when someone could not control what she said, it seems that the Rabbis of the Talmud would have preferred silence rather than empty-headed speech. "Rabban Shimon ben Gamliel taught, 'Throughout my life, I was raised among the scholars, and I discovered that there is nothing more becoming a person than silence . . . [for] excess in speech leads to sin.'" (Mishnah *Pirkei Avot* 1:17).

The Rabbis of the Talmud vied with each other in coining clever teachings to demonstrate just how terrible *Lashon HaRah* could be. One passage of the Talmud (Tractate *Arachin* 15b) contains a long list of these various rabbis' teachings. Here is a selection with explanations: "Rabbi Yochanon said in the name of Rabbi Yosef ben Zimra, 'Whoever bears evil tales will be visited by the plague of leprosy, as it is said, "Whoever slanders his neighbor in secret, him I will destroy [through leprosy]."'" (Psalms 101:5)

Rabbi Yochanon interprets this verse from Psalms to mean that God will destroy one who slanders his neighbor through the plague of leprosy. The Rabbis drew a connection between slander and the plague of leprosy from the Torah story where Miriam, Moses' older sister, spoke ill of Moses for having married a Cushite woman. God punished Miriam by inflicting her with leprosy, however she was ultimately healed when

Moses prayed to God on her behalf. (Numbers, Chapter 12) "Resh Lakish said, 'One who slanders causes his sin to reach to the heavens, as it is said, "They have set their mouth against the heavens, and their tongue walks through the earth."'" (Psalms 73:9) The walking tongue referred to in this Psalm is tantamount to slander according to Resh Lakish. Therefore, the mouths of those who slander is set against and even reaches up to the heavens in its destructive aftermath.

> Rabbi Hisda said in the name of Mar Ukba, "Regarding one who slanders, the Holy One, blessed be He, says, 'He and I cannot live together in this world.' As it is said, 'Whoever slanders his neighbor in secret, him I will destroy; whoever is haughty of the eye and proud in the heart, him will I not suffer.' (Psalms 101:5) Don't read the [Hebrew word as if it says] "*him* will I not suffer," rather, read it as if it said, "*with* him [In which case, the verse can be read as if it meant:] I will not suffer [to dwell together with] him."

Rabbi Hisda bases his teaching on a Hebrew word pun. Because Hebrew is not written with vowels, the consanants of any given word can be pronounced differently to yield an entirely different word. Rather than reading the verse from Psalms as if it simply said, "him I will not suffer" (meaning "to tolerate"), Rabbi Hisda re-read the Hebrew word as it if meant, "*with* him I will not suffer." In other words, Rabbi Hisda suggests God is saying, "this world is not big enough for both Me and a slanderer!"

> Rabba said, "He who wants to live [can find life] through the tongue, and he wants to die [can find death] through the tongue . . ." (*Tractate Arachin* 15b)
>
> In [the land of Israel] the rabbis used to say, "Talking about another person [who is not there] kills three people—the one who tells [the story], the one who hears it, and the one about whom it is being told." (*Tractate Arachin* 15b)
>
> Rabbi Hama ben Hanina said, "What is the meaning of this verse, 'Death and life are in the hand [i.e. the power] of the tongue?' (Proverbs 18:21) Does a tongue have a 'hand'? Rather, it tells us that just as the hand can kill, so too can the tongue [through gossip]." (*Tractate Arachin* 15b)
>
> Rabba said, "Whoever wants to live [can find life] through the tongue [through the study of the Torah]. But whoever wants to die [can find death] through the tongue [through gossip]." (*Tractate Arachin* 15b)

This last group of short passages indicates the far-reaching and socially destructive nature of *Lashon HaRah*. Social discourse can ruin people's reputations and kill them in their community. Thus, *Lashon HaRah* is equated with death. However, the power of speech is also equated with life, for whoever studies the Torah and teaches it thereby uses their tongue to spread the knowledge of the Torah, the source of Jewish life.

While all of the Rabbis were clearly in agreement about the terrible nature of speaking inappropriate language, they did not define what actually constitutes gossip with any degree of clarity. This task was tackled by Rabbi Moses Maimonides—a rabbi who lived in Egypt in the twelfth century—in his important work of Jewish law entitled the Mishneh Torah. The Rambam (acronym for Maimonides) clearly and precisely defined three forms of gossip which he labeled *Rechilut* (which literally means "tale bearer," with tale referring to unsubstantiated derogatory information), *Lashon HaRah* (which literally means "evil tongue" and refers to derogatory information that is true) and *Motzi shem rah* (which literally means, "bringing forth a bad name" and refers to derogatory information that is false). The Rambam wrote in the Mishneh Torah:

> What is *Rechilut*—a gossiper? This is someone who claims things [about someone else] and goes from this one to this one and says, "I heard this about so-and-so; I heard that about such-and-such " Even though this may be the truth, behold, it still destroys the [fabric] of the [social] world.

> There is a sin even worse than this and it is *Lashon HaRah*—"evil speech." It is one who recounts [something] derogatory about his fellow person even though he is speaking the truth!
>
> But the one who recounts lies [about his fellow] is called, *Motzi shem rah*—one who spreads an evil name. [Mishneh Torah, *Hilchot Deot* 7:2]

Despite the pervasive nature of gossip, and despite the fact that many people enjoy speaking about other people's business—whether true or false and whether derogatory or not—it is clear from the passages in the Torah, the Talmud, and the Mishneh Torah, that this form of speech is prohibited according to the Jewish tradition. So what can we talk about? That is the challenge we all face.

It is probably not too great an exaggeration to claim that perhaps half of our daily speech is forbidden under one or more, if not all, of the three forbidden forms of speech. But not all cases are so easy to judge. Consider the following situations and decide for yourself whether each case involves *Lashon HaRah*, *Rechilut*, *Motzi shem rah*, or none of these. What would you do if you were to confront these situations in reality?

1. You saw someone passing around someone else's note or letter. *Is this forbidden in the Jewish tradition?*

2. You overheard the sharing of negative information about someone which was common knowledge. *Is that wrong?*
3. You overheard the sharing of private information. *Was this wrong? And what would you do?*
4. You heard someone make a negative statement about someone else, but they included themselves in the same derogatory statement. *Does this make it okay?*
5. Someone divulged to you a friend's confessions of wrong-doing. *Is listening to this kind of information considered* Lashon HaRah?
6. Someone related negative information about someone else while in the presence of that very person. *Do you think it's considered* Lashon HaRah *to share these comments in front of the very person they're about?*
7. Someone was making negative statements about other people but in jest. *Does this make it acceptable?*
8. You were in a small crowd and heard someone relay negative information about someone else. *Does being in a crowd make a difference?*
9. Someone shared ambiguously negative information. *If the information is questionable, does that make it any better?*
10. Someone relayed negative information but did not mention any names. *Does anonymity mitigate this situation?*

Despite the prevalence of such social situations, the Jewish tradition prohibits all of the circumstances above and declares them to be forms of *Lashon HaRah*, or forbidden speech.

The Hofetz Hayyim, the pen name for Rabbi Yisrael Meir Kagen, was a Russian rabbi who died in 1933. His great expertise was in the area of Jewish law related to *Lashon HaRah*, and he wrote many books about all of the specific do's and don't's relating to gossip. Legend says he once tried to convince a Jewish businessman to buy and read some of his books on *Lashon HaRah*. The businessman kept refusing. He finally explained that he could not buy any the books because in his line of work, it was necessary for him to engage in *Lashon HaRah* in order to do business, and therefore, maintain his livelihood. Undeterred, the Hofetz Hayyim replied, "That may be so, but you should still buy my books on *Lashon HaRah* if for no other reason that you will read them and then sigh [in sadness about not being able to observe the prohibition against speaking *Lashon HaRah*]." Perhaps the Hofetz Hayyim meant that even though the businessman could not observe the laws against *Lashon HaRah* at the present moment, such knowledge could ultimately lead to his future observance.

There are many possible responses to *Lashon HaRah*. One can walk away, one can actively change the subject, or one can also rebuke their friends and acquaintances as a way to try and expand their awareness and sensitivity to the subject. However, the challenge of rebuking someone in an appropriate way can be quite complicated and demanding. Therefore, the Jewish tradition has much advice to offer in this area.

2

Rebuking Your Fellow Person

Many people have problems dealing with their feelings of anger. When frustrated, some people may either overreact, expressing an inappropriate amount of hostility, or in contrast, try to suppress their volatile emotions. Rarely do we encounter people who, being in constant harmony with their inner emotional state, are able to express their feelings of animosity in a sensitive, healthy, and even effective manner. As difficult and as challenging as this last option may be to master, this is the path that the Jewish tradition encourages us to follow.

Based on the previous chapter dealing with gossip, consider how you might respond to the following situation:

> You overhear some people talking about you and hear them say that a friend of yours, or a co-worker,

had said something untrue about you. What would you do? Some options that you may consider could be to:

- Enter the conversation and deny the allegations.
- Try and ignore the conversation and act normally but secretly harbor animosity towards your friend or co-worker.
- Try to act normally but plan to wreak vengeance upon your friend or co-worker in some other way.
- Spread an equally untrue and hurtful rumor about your friend or co-worker.
- Make an honest attempt to turn the other cheek and stay friends with your friend or co-worker by ignoring the incident.
- Do nothing but later confront your friend or co-worker regarding the incident in private.

There is no right or wrong response to this hypothetical situation. Rather, each option carries its own consequences, both positive or negative. For example, entering the conversation may cause the other people to feel uncomfortable and lead them to change the subject in your presence. Defending yourself may convince people of your innocence although it would be difficult to know for sure. However, such strategies may also backfire, leading others to question your sincerity and end up strengthening their feelings of ambivalence towards you.

The focus of Jewish tradition, however, is not upon what other people think about you, but rather, on how you should handle it. In situations like this one, sometimes not expressing one's feelings can cause a minor annoyance or sense of injustice to fester and turn into something far more destructive, such as anger and hatred. The Torah actually provides explicit advice regarding these kinds of situations. Leviticus 19:17–18 lays out the general principle regarding dealing with anger:

> You shall not hate your fellow person in your heart.
> Reprove your fellow
> but incur no guilt because of him.
> You shall not take vengeance
> or bear a grudge against your countryman.
> Love your fellow as yourself:
> I am the LORD.

These verses in the Torah are not placed in this sequence haphazardly. Rather, they can be understood to form a flowchart of behavior and consequences. "You shall not hate your fellow person in your heart" is not couched in a specific context. Rather, the Torah focuses directly upon us and our potential feelings of anger toward a friend, family member, or co-worker. However, the Torah challenges us with a demanding requirement; despite what we might feel, we are not permitted to hate this person quietly, in our hearts. Yet, this is almost an unrealistic expectation of human beings. We often cannot control what we feel inside ourselves. We feel whatever we may happen to feel!

Such a situation could be intolerable. Therefore, the next clause of this same verse in the Torah addresses this issue: "Reprove your fellow but incur no guilt because of him." Rather than bottle up our feelings of anger or hatred, the Torah demands that we express our feelings, not by shouting or taking vengeance, but rather, by directly confronting the person towards whom we are harboring animosity. In the best of all possible worlds, what they said or did could have been a mistake and they really intended no harm or insult towards us. In this case, our anger would prove unwarranted. Ideally, our fellow person, once confronted with our hurt and anger, may choose to apologize, thereby creating a sense of closure to this episode.

However, this verse in the Torah does not end there. It continues with a tantalizingly ambiguous phrase— "Incur no guilt because of him" This is a difficult clause and we will deal with it in greater depth later. However, one possible explanation for this verse is that it refers back to the commandment to rebuke a fellow person. To what extent can or should we rebuke someone else? Even to the point of embarrassing them and causing them pain and shame? The Talmud asserts that there is indeed a limit to this commandment: if we inadvertently humiliate or hurt the person we are rebuking, then we are guilty of continuing this cycle of wounded feelings. Therefore, this clause is a warning for us to curb our zeal while reprimanding others.

The next verse then warns us of the deleterious consequences of not fulfilling the commandment to rebuke our fellow person: "You shall not take vengeance or bear a grudge against your countryman." If we avoid rebuking our friends, our anger and hatred may build up to such an extent that we try to take vengeance against them or bear a grudge toward them, which may ultimately lead to further anger or violence. The danger of trying to keep angry feelings inside is that they will eventually express themselves, whether internally, by making our bodies sick, or externally, manifesting themselves in socially destructive behavior. For this reason the Torah places the verses in this order. Seeking vengeance or bearing a grudge is a logical potential consequence of not rebuking our fellow person when warranted.

The goal of this cycle of hurt feelings and censure is not to hate our fellow people, friends, family members or co-workers, but ultimately to love them. As the Torah verse says, "Love your fellow as yourself: I am the Lord." This is the ideal outcome of this flowchart of actions and consequences. If we can successfully deal with our anger, we may avoid hatred in our hearts by seeking a healthy and appropriate confrontation with our fellow person. This in turn, will enable us to restore harmony to our societal relationships which is what the Torah seeks to create.

The Talmud helps shed some additional light on these verses from the Torah. The following passage reveals how the Rabbis in ancient times understood these verses from the Torah dealing with anger and rebuking others.

> It was taught: "You shall not hate your kinsfolk." From this it would be possible to [narrowly] conclude that you may not merely hit, strike, or curse your fellow person! Therefore, [to expand this understanding] the text also states, "in your heart." That is, the Torah is speaking about [harboring] hatred in your heart. (Tractate *Arachin* 16b)

The Rabbis point out here that one possible motivation to rebuke our fellow person may be to attempt to purge our own heart of anger, irrespective of whether it has socially beneficial consequences. The Talmud continues and explains an unusual Hebrew phrase in these Torah verses, deriving additional meaning and significance from them.

> From where do we know that if a person sees something unseemly [indecent or inappropriate] in his neighbor, he is obligated to rebuke him? Because

> the Torah states, "Reprove your kinsman." But if he rebuked him and he did not accept, where do we know that he must rebuke him yet again? Because the text states, "surely rebuke" meaning, in all ways possible. (Tractate *Arachin* 16)

In the Hebrew, the word *rebuke* appears twice in this phrase and is translated as, "surely rebuke," in order to emphasize the commandment. Therefore, this passage implies that an additional motivation to rebuke one's fellow is to seek the improvement of our fellow human being. The passage continues in reference to this emphasis on rebuking: "One might assume [that this obligation to continue to rebuke applies] even if his face becomes pales [through shame or embarrassment]! Therefore the text states, 'but incur no guilt because of him.'"

The purpose of rebuking one's fellow is both egocentric and altruistic. On one hand, we try to unburden our own heart of our angry feelings and on the other, we seek to possibly improve the ways of someone else. We also learn another possible meaning of the curious phrase—"Incur no guilt because of him"—that the Talmud clearly sees as a caution regarding how to reprove someone else. If we get carried away in our zeal and enthusiasm in rebuking our fellow person, we may end up committing a new transgression, namely, embarrassing our fellow person. Therefore, rebuking someone is an act which requires sensitivity and tact.

But what is the best way to fulfill this commandment to rebuke our fellow person? The Torah provides us with few clues. Fortunately, Rabbi Moses Maimonides (Rambam) provides us with a clear and detailed set of instructions in this sensitive matter:

> When a person sins against another person—he should not hate him and be silent . . . rather, it is a commandment to inform his fellow and say, "Why have you done such and such against me?" For it says, "You shall reprove your kinsmen." And if he repents and requests forgiveness, you must grant it to him. And the one who forgives should not be cruel [and not forgive him].
>
> The one who reproves his friend should rebuke him in private and speak to him calmly and with soft language. If he accepts your words—good. But if not, you should rebuke him a second and third time. . . . Whoever has the opportunity to prevent the commission of a crime and does not do so, will be held accountable for this crime himself.
>
> The one who reproves his friend the first time should not speak to him harshly or shame him, for it says, "Incur no guilt because of him." So too, did the sages say, "whoever shames his friend in public has no share in the World to Come." Therefore, a person should be careful not to embarrass his friend in public.

> If a person's friend committed a transgression against him and this person does not want to rebuke his friend or even say anything about it . . . because he might cause this friend to do again or provoke him to do something worse . . . and if [despite all of this] this person can sincerely forgive his friend and not hate him secretly—this is an example of true piety. [Mishneh Torah, *Hilchot Deot*, 6:6–9]

The Rambam provides a great deal of practical advice as to how to fulfill the potentially disastrous commandment of reproving our fellow person. First, he reminds us that when we rebuke others, if they immediately see the error of their ways and request forgiveness, we should not be stubborn, but be merciful and forgiving. Secondly, Rambam advises us to rebuke in private—so as not to publicly embarrass someone—to pick our words carefully, and to speak in an appropriate, soft tone of voice. Afterall, the point is to be heard, not to grandstand. But if a rebuke is not accepted, we have an obligation to continue our efforts to speak to this person. Clearly this is a situation where the motivation is not merely to exorcise our own feelings of anger, but to effect a positive change in the other person. Rambam makes this point poignantly when he asserts that by failing to rebuke someone when they have done wrong is tantamount to being held as guilty as if we ourselves had committed the same offense.

Rambam's words provide a second possible meaning

to the phrase, "Incur no guilt because of him." When emphasizing the importance of this commandment to rebuke a fellow person, Rambam emphasizes that should someone fail to rebuke their fellow person for whatever reason—be it lack of courage, fear, or apathy—then that person will be held just as morally responsible as the person who should have been rebuked. In other words, there is no difference in this case between a sin of commission and a sin of omission.

The second verse from the Torah passage above contains the commandment prohibiting us from seeking vengeance and bearing a grudge against someone else. But just what do these terms mean and what is the difference between them? The Talmud provides a context and definitions for these actions:

> What does the verse, "You shall not take vengeance or bear a grudge against your countryman," mean? It refers to monetary matters, as it was taught: What is vengeance? What is bearing a grudge?
>
> Vengeance is if person A says to person B, "Lend me your sickle," and person B replies, "No." The next day, person B says to person A, "Lend me your ax," and person A says, "I will not lend to you just as you did not lend to me!" This is vengeance.
>
> Bearing a grudge is when person A says to person B, "Lend me your ax," and person B says, "No." The

next day, person B says to person A, "Lend me your cloak," and person A replies, "Here it is. I am not like you who would not lend!" This is bearing a grudge.

[Might these refer to] Actual physical pain? No. [Tractate *Yoma* 23a]

It is interesting to note that the Talmud does not assume that vengeance and bearing a grudge refer to physical acts of violence, but rather to the world of everyday life and interactions. The Talmud clearly specifies that vengeance is an action of reprisal accompanied by verbal explanation. It is the desire to retaliate joined with action. Whereas bearing a grudge is a verbal assault with no act of reprisal. The desire to retaliate is still there but is not acted upon. Therefore it is only verbal retaliation. In a world such as ours where the terms "vengeance" and "bearing a grudge" often have horrific connotations of violence, it is perhaps a relief to see that the Jewish tradition relegates such acts to a more benign world of mere social tension.

The Rambam, however, raised a possibility not covered by the Torah or the Talmud. That is, what if we are unable to rebuke our fellow person because we know that our rebuke will either only cause the other person to transgress further by provoking or enraging them, or that our words will simply be ignored? If these are the only possible outcomes that we anticipate, what should we do? Do we still have the obligation to rebuke or should we drop the subject? The Talmud provides some surprising answers:

> There are three [types of people] whom God loves: whoever doesn't become angry; whoever doesn't get drunk; and whoever doesn't stand on their own dignity. There are three [types of people] whom God hates: whoever says one thing with his mouth but thinks another in his heart; whoever knows exculpatory information about a friend but does not testify on his behalf; whoever sees a debased quality in their friend but testifies against him singly. [Tractate *Pesachim* 113b]

The background for this last statement is that in the Jewish legal tradition, a single witness is by definition not believed by a court of law. In fact, when a single witness steps forward with negative information about someone, this can only lead to *Motzi shem rah*—that is, spreading a bad reputation about that person. It does so because it raises the question of why the witness did not rebuke the person in private in the first place, but waited to present his negative testimony in a court of law?

It is also important to note that such hyperbolic statements in the Talmud about whom God may love or hate are exactly that—exaggerations. The Rabbis of the Talmud often resort to hyperbole in order to emphasize important moral qualities which they either want to encourage or eliminate. The last point of this passage is significant in our context of rebuking someone. The Rabbis wanted to encourage the performance of this commandment to the point of claiming that whoever does not rebuke their fellow person is hated by God! Strong words indeed, but we must remember that the Rabbis did not know anything more or less about God than any other human being. Rather, these statements were expressions of the value-system of the Rabbis and should be understood from that mitigating point of view. The talmudic passage continues with additional details about this last point:

> Once, Tuvia sinned and Zigud came alone and testified against him before Rav Papa, who then punished Zigud. [Zigud] said to [Rav Papa], "Tuvia sinned and I get punished?!" [Rav Papa] replied, "Yes! For it is written, 'A single witness may not give testimony.' (Deuteronomy 19:15) Yet, you came alone and testified against [Tuvia]—therefore, all you merely succeeded in doing was to spread a malicious rumor about him!" (Tractate *Pesachim* 113b)

Rav Papa was making a point that no legal action or punishment can be enacted on the basis of the testimony of a single witness. Therefore, even when someone chooses not to rebuke someone or for some other reason is unable to do so, they also cannot tell others about it because a single witness is not considered reliable. The Rabbis discussed the implications of this situation in the continuation of the passage:

> Rabbi Shmuel Bar Yitzhak said in the name of Rav: "[If you cannot rebuke someone and you cannot testify against them] it is permitted to hate them! As it says, 'When you see the ass of your *enemy* lying under its burden. . . .' (Exodus 23:5)" [The Talmud then asks] Which "enemy" is meant [in this verse]? Perhaps we can say it refers to an "enemy" who is a non-Jew?! [No, we cannot, because] it was taught: An "enemy" here is obviously referring to a Jew! (Tractate *Pesachim* 113b)

The Talmud often gives incomplete quotes precisely when the point it is trying to make is left unquoted. Therefore, the point that is being made here relies on the rest of this verse which states in its entirety, "When you see the ass of your enemy lying under its burden, you must nevertheless raise it with him." In other words, one must even help his enemy when his enemy's animal is in distress. For reasons which may seem obscure, the Rabbis declared that the enemy referred to in this verse is a fellow Jew. Although the logic is faint here, the Talmud claims that the assumed context of the biblical verse is that if someone's enemy was not Jewish, the Torah would have explicitly said that. Because the Torah does not specify in the verse above that the enemy is not Jewish, the Talmud assumes that he must be a Jew.

Since the Torah refers to a fellow Jew as someone's enemy, the Rabbis suggest in this passage that it is permitted to think of someone as an enemy, that is, someone whom it is acceptable to hate. The apparent digression is necessary because the context of the original verses in Leviticus about rebuking your fellow person refer, in fact, to another Jew. Therefore, the Talmud goes out of its way to prove that the enemy in this other verse quoted in the passage above must also be a Jew.

It may seem parochial and narrow-minded of the Rabbis, and perhaps even the Torah, to limit the scope of these commandments to only other Jews. After all, part of the moral power of the Torah is its assertion of the absolute equality of all human beings who are created in the image of God. Both the Torah and Talmud, however, reflect their own historically and culturally entrenched viewpoints. Perhaps it is unfair to demand a higher moral perspective of the very texts which enabled the Jewish people to embrace a greater, universal human perspective of the world. However, it could be argued that a universal perspective of humanity must be grounded in a particular culture and tradition. Therefore, it is of great value to follow the logical, developmental steps of the Rabbis' arguments as examples which provided future generations of

Jews with the tools through which to adopt a far more universal and accepting moral philosophy.

The Talmud continues to pursue this issue of whether one is allowed to hate someone else, in a manner contrary to what we have seen the Torah says. In fact, the Talmud points out this very contradiction:

> But is it really permitted to hate this person [the enemy Jew in the Torah]?! What about what is written, "You shall not hate your fellow in your heart" (Leviticus 19:17)?! If there were other witnesses that this person committed some transgression, then indeed, everyone should hate him! However, [referring to the enemy in the Torah whose ass falls over due to its burden], why [should the person in the Torah] come to hate *this* particular person [referred to as his enemy]? Because he saw in him something indecent or inappropriate. (Tractate *Pesachim* 113b)

In other words, the Talmud hints at the circumstances which might induce someone to rebuke his fellow person—namely, if he saw qualities in him that were indecent or inappropriate. If there is such a person and one either cannot or does not rebuke him, is it still permitted for one to hate this person in her heart without rebuking him? This extended talmudic passage finally ends with the surprising conclusion: "Rav Nahman Bar Yitzhak said, 'It is a commandment to hate him! As it says, "Fearing the Lord is to hate evil."'"

(Proverbs 8:13). [Tractate *Pesachim* 113b] The ramifications of this talmudic passage are disturbing because it implies that not only is it permitted to hate someone who cannot be rebuked or testified against, but the Talmud positively commands it! However, it should be clear from the extenuating circumstances of this unusual situation that this case is exceptional. The practical implications of this passage are that the only situation in which the biblical prohibition not to hate one's fellow in one's heart can be waived are when we never reveal our hatred and never act upon it. This, however, would seem to negate one of the very premises for rebuking one's fellow person—to try to expunge these feelings of hatred from our heart!

Rather than nurse such a hatred forever with no possibility of relief, the Talmud, in another passage, ultimately suggests a much healthier solution as to how to end this vicious cycle: "Rabba said, 'Whoever does not stand on his own qualities (wounded pride) has all his transgressions passed over by God.'" (Tractate *Yoma* 23a) Whoever voluntarily abstains from rebuking someone, who either cannot or will not react appropriately to being rebuked, will find an outlet for their anger and pain through God. If all of the suggestions specified in Leviticus 19:17–18 should break down or prove untenable, then the only course of action we have to break the cycle of hatred is forgiveness. If we can forgo our own anger and hatred, then the Talmud assures us, our own flaws and transgressions will be forgiven by God.

However, it is not always possible to overcome our own feelings of anger, whether we rebuke someone else to ameliorate our wounded feelings, or we bottle them up inside of ourselves. Anger will always find a way to express itself. The Jewish tradition is familiar with anger—both human and divine—and is replete with examples of what to avoid.

3

Dealing with Anger

The Jewish tradition is quite familiar with the effects of anger, both human and divine. The Torah is filled with examples of how human anger leads to terrible and destructive consequences. Although the Torah never explicitly declares that anger is an inappropriate or ruinous emotional reaction, the context of each story clearly reveals that this is indeed the Torah's point of view. Beginning immediately after creation, the Torah relates stories of anger and destruction. Despite the fact that both Cain and Abel made offerings to God, God did not accept them equally.

> But to Cain and his offering, [God] paid no heed. Cain was much distressed and his face fell. And the Lord said to Cain, "Why are you distressed, and why is your face fallen? Surely if you do right, there is uplift. But if you do not do right, sin crouches at the door; its urge is toward you yet you can be its master." [Genesis 4:5–9]

This is an unusual situation in the Torah. Clearly, for reasons unknown to Cain, and perhaps even to us, God refused to acknowledge Cain's offering to God. This caused Cain much anguish, and as we already know, so much anger that he eventually expressed it through fratricide. God even comments upon Cain's "fallen face" and issues an oblique warning regarding sin and its "urge." Perhaps the Torah is implying that this "urge" is anger, or that doing evil is motivated by anger. It is also unclear if God already knows about or anticipates the murder of Abel. The Torah is notoriously and frustratingly silent in such cases. Yet, God offers a tantalizing hint that despite sin's urge being towards us—that is, despite the power that our destructive and self-destructive emotions may have over us—it is possible to master them and maintain control. However, Cain was either unwilling or unable to do so.

Later on in the Torah, intra-family animosity once again leads to murderous intentions among Jacob's many sons: "And when [Joseph's] brothers saw that their father [Jacob] loved him more than any of his brothers, they hated him so that they could not speak a friendly word to him." (Genesis 37:4) The jealousy that Joseph's brothers experienced was later expressed in their desire to kill their younger brother. However, they were later persuaded to sell him into slavery instead. Perhaps if the brothers had been able to live by the Torah's commandment of not harboring hatred in one's heart, they might have overcome their jealousy. Maybe this commandment in Leviticus was motivated by a memory of this story in which the older brothers could not even bring themselves to utter a single word to Joseph, whether good or bad. Instead of expressing themselves, they kept their anger inside, where it festered and later lead to violence.

Even Moses, the greatest of the prophets in the Torah and the archetype of leadership, proved unable to restrain his anger and lead him to murder.

> He [Moses] saw an Egyptian beating a Hebrew, one of his kinsmen. He turned this way and that and seeing no one about, he struck down the Egyptian and buried him in the sand. When he went out the next day, he found two Hebrews fighting; so he said to the offender, "Why do you strike your fellow?" He retorted, "Who made you chief and ruler over us? Do you mean to kill me as you killed the Egyptian?" [Exodus 2:11–14]

This episode is filled with delicious irony and foreshadows Moses' later career. It is no accident that his first activity in the Torah was motivated by anger. Even though he was raised in Pharaoh's court, Moses seems to have always known that he was a Hebrew, as indicated above, and he seems to have always had a passion for justice. In this case, his passion—perhaps anger over injustice—led him to commit a premeditated murder. After all, it says that Moses first carefully looked around to see if he could get away with it, and then tried to hide the evidence of the crime by burying the body in the sand. Appropriately, Moses was drawn to intervene when other Israelites were expressing their anger, apparently through fighting. How ironic that Moses tried to chastise the two Hebrews for acting on their anger, exactly as Moses himself had done previously! He was then even taunted by the Hebrews for his hypocrisy. One of the purposes of this scene is to foreshadow Moses' eventual leadership over the Hebrews, placed there by God, and Moses continual need to justify his authority.

Perhaps this story also presages Moses' difficulty with controlling his own anger later on in his career. For Moses' last sin was the same as his first—acting on his anger. Towards the end of the desert wanderings, Moses is commanded to speak to a rock to bring forth water.

> Moses took the rod from before the Lord, as He had commanded him. Moses and Aaron assembled the congregation in front of the rock; and he said to them, "Listen, you rebels, shall we get water for you out of this rock?" And Moses raised his hand and struck the rock twice with his rod. Out came copious water, and the community and their animals drank. But the Lord said to Moses and Aaron, "Because you

> did not trust Me enough to affirm My sanctity in the sight of the Israelite people, therefore you shall not lead this congregation into the land that I have given them." [Numbers 20:9–12]

Instead of following God's instructions to merely speak to the rock, Moses angrily denounced the Israelites, accusing them of rebelling against God's authority. Yet Moses himself then disobeyed God's authority and struck the rock. For this sin, Moses was condemned to not enter the promised land. How ironic—or perhaps consistent—that his career which began with a killing blow to an Egyptian ended with a blow to the rock, providing water, a life source to the people. Yet, it brought upon himself a sentence of death before he could lead the people into the promised land.

God's original advice to Cain—that human beings can master their feelings of anger—ultimately goes unheeded throughout the Torah. Because they were created with free will, God is powerless to prevent people from exercising their freedom of action, even when it will result in tragic consequences. Therefore, it is ironic that God cannot even manage to control His own anger throughout the stories of the Torah. Immediately after creation, because of violence and lawlessness, God regrets having created humanity: "And the Lord regretted that He had made man on earth, and His heart was saddened. The Lord said, 'I will blot out from the earth the men whom I created—men together with beasts, creeping things, and birds of the sky, for I regret that I made them.'" (Genesis 6:6) Although this sounds more like sadness than anger, God loses faith in human beings very quickly after having created them. After only a few short chapters in the beginning of Genesis, God expresses regret about having ever created them in the first place. There must be some anger behind God's intentions, or why would he destroy all of the non-human species as well? Only the fish, Noah's family and his boatload of animals, survived this flood. It is curious that God immediately chose to annihilate humanity without even a second thought.

God's anger flares again when confronted with actual rebellion by the Israelites in the desert, which God interprets as being directed against God Himself. Speaking to Moses, God thunders: "Now, Let Me be that My anger may blaze forth against them and that I may destroy them, and make of you a great nation." (Exodus 32:10)

During the forty days and forty nights that Moses was with God on the top of Mt. Sinai, the people of Israel below fell into despair over Moses' fate and decided to create an idol of a calf made of gold and worship it. God, knowing everything, immediately informed Moses of these events and became incensed. God's first reaction was to destroy the Israelites and create a new nation through Moses, much as he had done with Noah and the flood. The only reason God did not destroy the Israelites was due to Moses' intervention, which assuaged God's wrath. Based on the stories of the Torah, it seems that God has a recurring desire to destroy His own handiwork and start all over again whenever things begin to go wrong.

This is clear from God's reaction to other incidents of rebellion and complaining by the Israelites while wandering in the desert: "And the Lord said to Moses, 'How long will this people spurn Me, and how long will they have no faith in Me despite all the signs that I have performed in their midst? I will strike them with pestilence and disown them, and I will make of you a nation far more numerous than they!'" (Numbers 14:11–12) God grew angry with the Israelites after they believed the inaccurate report of the Israelite spies sent to search out the promised land. Upon hearing the news that they would not be able to overcome the native inhabitants, the Israelites despaired of being able to conquer and enter the promised land. God understood this, appropriately enough, as a loss of faith in Him and in His power to do anything within the divine will. Once again, His first instinctual reaction was to get mad and want to destroy the Israelites, beginning again with Moses.

Through these stories about Moses and God, the Torah seems to highlight the negative, destructive consequences of anger. When human beings become angry, they end up committing murder or disobeying

God. And when God becomes angry, God becomes destructive, wiping out humanity in the flood, or expressing the desire to destroy the Israelites and start over again on several occasions. Through these narratives, the Torah enables readers to draw their own conclusions and moral lessons from these stories.

However, the Talmud is far more explicit and clear in its denunciation of the deleterious repercussions of anger. The Rabbis also noticed Moses' tendency to become angry. One Rabbi noticed at least three cases of Moses' anger in which he was clearly in the wrong: "Rabbi Elazar said, 'Three times did Moses come into the category of error because he gave way to anger. . . . Because he was enticed by his anger, he was lead to err.'" (Sifrei, Parashat Matot, Piska 5)

This midrash refers to the following stories in the Torah:

Moses scolds his brother Aaron for not carrying out an aspect of the sacrifices correctly because he when was still in shock after the death of his two oldest sons, Nadav and Abihu. When Aaron explains his reasons, Moses acquiesces, admitting he was at fault.

(Leviticus 10:16)

Moses hits the rock to produce water for the Israelites instead of speaking to it as God had commanded.

(Numbers 20:10)

Moses rebukes the army for sparing the lives of the women after defeating the Moabites. However, this was immediately contradicted by the high priest Elazar in Numbers 31:21.

(Numbers 31:14)

The Rabbis of the Talmud had nothing but scorn for those who lost their temper easily and gave way to anger. The Rabbis made the following comments about angry people, each time providing copious biblical support for their statement. Among their conclusions are:

> Rabba son of Rav Huna said, "Whoever loses his temper, even the Divine presence is unimportant in his eyes . . ."
>
> Rabbi Jeremiah of Difti said, "[The angry man] forgets his learning and becomes ever more stupid [the longer he remains angry] . . ."
>
> Rav Nachman son of Isaac said, "It is certain that [the angry man's sins] outnumber his merits, for it is written, 'An angry man provokes a quarrel, a hot-tempered man commits many offenses.'" (Proverbs 29:22) [Tractate *Nedarim* 22b]

The Rabbis worried about the stability of someone who was easily prone to anger. If they were unable to control themselves, they may not only commit minor offenses and religious transgressions, but possibly even major prohibitions of the Torah: "Rabbi Akiba said, 'Whoever tears his clothes and breaks his furniture in his passion and wrath will in the end become an idolater, for such is the craft of the evil inclination. Today it says, "Tear your clothes," and tomorrow it says, "Worship idols."'" (*Avot deRebbi Natan*, Chapter 3, 8a)

Not only does someone who lose their temper risk transgressing major tenets of Judaism, but they risk eschatological torments as well: "Whoever loses his temper is exposed to all of the torments of Gehenna, for it is written, 'Therefore remove anger from your heart, and [thus will you] put away evil from your flesh.'" (Ecclesiastes 11:10) (Tractate *Nedarim* 22a) The Rabbis understood this reference to evil to refer to Gehenna, a vague rabbinic concept similar to Purgatory—that is, a place of punishment and pain reserved for the wicked in this world. However, such suffering is only temporary in rabbinic theology. The way to avoid such afflication in the next world, according to this passage, is to avoid becoming angry in this world. The Rabbis urged people to control their passions, "Who is mighty? Whoever can conquer their inclinations [to become angry and thus lose control]." (Mishnah *Pirkei Avot* 4:1)

Rabbi Moses Maimonides clearly explains the proper emotional balance that all human beings should strive to achieve. Influenced by Aristotelian philosophy and emphasis upon moderation, Rambam wrote:

> The straight path is the middle quality among all of the possible qualities that a person has, and is the attitude which is the furthest from the extreme ends, and is not closer to this or to that end. Therefore, the early sages commanded that a person should continually weigh his attitudes and direct them in the "middle path" so that he should be complete and whole in his body.
>
> How so? He should not be "hot headed," easy to anger, nor should he be like a corpse, completely unfeeling. Rather, he should be in the middle, not getting angry, except for truly important things which are worth growing angry over. [Mishneh Torah, *Hilchot Deot* 1:4)

While Rambam advocated that we adhere to the middle road of moderation in our emotional life, he also acknowledged that anger can and even should play a role in our lives. However, rather than growing angry over trivial things, Rambam insisted that when we become angry, we should do so for significant and momentous matters in life. What they are, he declines to mention, and instead leaves that challenge for us to confront on our own.

However, it may happen that other people may decide that our actions are worthy targets of their anger, and decide to express their feelings through violence directed at us. When that happens, the Jewish tradition advocates acting in self-defense.

4

Self-defense

When words fail and anger flares, people often resort to expressing themselves through their fists, or knives, or guns. This phenomenon is the bane of our modern Western society. As Jews living in a Christian society, we are all familiar with the statement of Jesus—"If someone slaps you on the right cheek, turn and offer him your left." (Matthew 5:39) However, as Jews, our tradition does not demand submission or acceptance of violence. Instead, it enjoins us to defend ourselves.

The Hebrew Bible deals with the issue of self-defense in a number of widely scattered passages. Among the conclusions that can be gleaned from these verses are the following:

Deliberate homicide is absolutely forbidden by the Torah, because the blood of the victim stains and defiles both the land and the murderer. Murder leaves moral pollution in its wake. This is clear from the following verses dealing with murder:

> *[God speaks to Cain after the murder of Abel, saying,] "What have you done? Hark, your brother's blood cries out to Me from the ground!"*
>
> *(Genesis 4:10)*

> *[God tells the Israelites,] "You shall not pollute the land in which you live, for blood pollutes the land, and the land can have no expiation for blood that is shed on it, except by the blood of him who sheds it."*
>
> *(Numbers 35:33)*

The penalty for premeditated murder is capital punishment, because murder is tantamount to destruction of the divine image. The Torah states this very clearly a number of times:

> *[God tells Noah after the flood,] "For your own life-blood I will require a recokoning: I will require it of every . . . man, too, will I require a reckoning for human life, of every man for that of his fellow man! Whoever sheds the blood of man, by man shall his blood be shed; for in His image did God make man."*
>
> *(Genesis 9:5–6)*

> *[God commands the Israelites,] "He who fatally strikes a man shall be put to death."*
>
> *(Exodus 21:12)*

Even in the absence of humanly ordained punishment for murder, God will demand and ensure punishment for the murderers. The passages below speak about God holding human beings responsible for the death of others.

> *[God, speaking through the prophet Ezekiel, says metaphorically,] "But if the watchman sees the sword advancing and does not blow the horn, so that the people are not warned, and the sword comes and destroys one of them, that person was destroyed for his own sins; however, I will demand a reckoning for his blood from the watchman [who did not defend the people]."*
>
> *(Ezekiel 33:6)*

> *[God, speaking through the prophet Elisha, commands the army commander, Jehu,] "You shall strike down the House of Ahab your master; thus will I avenge on Jezebel the blood of My servants the prophets, and the blood of the other servants of the Lord."*
>
> *(II Kings 9:7)*

Accidental homicide (manslaughter) results in the killer having to flee to a city of refuge and remain there for his own safety to protect him from the blood-avenger. Vengeance is permitted in this case, but the manslaughter also has the right to defend himself:

> *[God commands the Israelites saying,] "You shall provide yourselves with places to serve you as cities of*

refuge to which a manslayer who has killed a person unintentionally may flee . . . from the blood-avenger so that the manslayer may not die unless he has stood trial before the assembly."

(Numbers 35:11–12)

"But if the manslayer ever goes outside the limits of the city of refuge to which he has fled, and the blood-avenger comes upon him . . . and kills the manslayer, there is no bloodguilt on his account."

(Numbers35:26–7)

[Parallels to the passages above are found in Deuteronomy 4:41–3 and 10:1–13]

However, manslaughter in the act of self-defense does not incur bloodguilt. The following passage is dealt with in great detail by the Rabbis of the Talmud and is the main focus of our discussion:

[God tells the Israelites,] "If the thief is seized while tunneling [under a wall for housebreaking] and he is beaten to death, there is no bloodguilt [upon the home-owner] in his case."

(Exodus 22:1)

While it is clearly forbidden to murder another person, the Torah does allow for the possibility of manslaughter during self defense. In this last case, if a home-owner discovers an intruder attempting to sneak into his home and in the act of defending his home and life he ends up killing the intruder, there is no bloodguilt upon the homeowner. Although technically translated as "tunneling" above, the Hebrew word used can also be understood to mean, "sneaking in." The reason that the homeowner incurs no bloodguilt is that it was not clear whether the intruder had come to steal or to murder.

The Talmud discusses this situation at length and delineates a special category of people in which it is acceptable to use violence against when in the cause of self-defense, referred to in Hebrew as rodef—"one who pursues":

> "If a thief is found breaking in . . ." (Exodus 22:1) [The Rabbis explain that] From this verse I only know that the law applies to a case of breaking into a person's home. How do I know that it might apply to [a case where the thief was found] on the roof, or in a courtyard, or an attached enclosure? Because the verse continues, ". . . wherever the thief is *found* . . ." (Exodus 22:3) implying wherever he is found as a thief. [The Rabbis challenge their own assertion] If so, then why does the verse state "tunneling in [to someone's house]"? Because his breaking in constitutes a formal warning [that is, the homeowner need not warn the thief before killing him]. [Tractate *Sanhedrin* 72b]

This passage expands a narrow understanding of the dispensation to allow for manslaughter in the case of a thief sneaking into one's home. The Talmud concludes from another verse dealing with the case of a thief that no matter where a thief might be found breaking into one's home—either through tunneling under a wall, or via the roof, or through a courtyard—if the homeowner finds him and kills him, then there is no bloodguilt upon the homeowner. "Bloodguilt" is simply the formal Jewish legal term used to refer to whether a person can be held liable for murder.

The Talmud, however, challenges its own logic and asks, if the above is indeed the case, why did the Torah specify that this thief should be discovered while "tunneling" or "sneaking in" if this guilt-free form of manslaughter applies to all methods of entry? The Talmud concludes that by sneaking in the thief forfeited any right to be warned that what he was doing could lead to his death.

The Talmud is speaking here rather elliptically about a kind of Miranda rights clause applicable to situations of potentially justifiable manslaughter during self-defense. This guilt-free case of manslaughter only applies, according to the Talmud, if a defender first warns his attacker that he faces death if he presses his attack. If the attacker ignores this warning and then ends up being killed, then obviously the defender is not guilty of murder, only manslaughter.

The Talmud, however, worries about this case from the Torah because there is no mention of the thief first being warned that he might be killed for breaking in! This is why the Talmud ultimately concludes that the act of sneaking in constitutes his formal warning. This means that by sneaking in he has formally waived his right to be warned before he is killed. In this way the Talmud places the blame for this death back upon the thief.

Having raised this topic of committing manslaughter without forewarning, the Talmud continues in a similar vein to strengthen the argument above even further:

> Rav Huna said, "A minor [a child below the age of Bar Mitzvah, 13 years old] who *pursues* [another person with murderous intent] may be killed to save the pursued." [The Talmud then explains] This is because he held that a pursuer [a *rodef*] does not need a warning, and it makes no difference whether the pursuer is a minor or an adult. (Tractate *Sanhedrin* 72b)

Extending the principle derived from the initial passage, Rav Huna asserts that anyone who pursues another with any sort of murderous intent, may be killed without first being warned. The fact that Rav Huna even specified that this applies to a minor emphasizes the latitude to which he was willing to extend this dispensation of killing a pursuer without forewarning. However, not everyone agreed with Rav Huna's logic:

> Rav Hisda objected and asked Rav Huna [regarding his opinion that killing a pursuer requires no warning], "[How do you respond to this following teaching which contradicts you?] It was taught that once [a baby's] head has come out [of the birth canal], it may not be harmed? Because [don't we already hold the principle that] one life may not take precedence over another life? Why not [go ahead and kill the baby]? After all, isn't it a [minor] *rodef*?!" (Tractate *Sanhedrin* 72b)

Rav Hisda objected to Rav Huna's "no warning needed" opinion based on a principle derived from a case of an abortion. A fetus may indeed be aborted in the Jewish tradition throughout pregnancy up to the beginning of the birth process. However, the moment the baby's head is free of the birth canal, abortions are no longer permitted. The reason is because of the principle, "One life may not take precedence over another life." Up until the baby's head is clear, the life of the fetus is not considered a life with all of the rights and privileges of a human being, who has already been born. Those rights, however, devolve to the baby the moment its head comes out. At this point, it becomes a full human being—indeed, a minor—and therefore, it cannot be aborted, for that would constitute murder.

Based on Rav Huna's daring assertion that even a minor can be considered a *rodef* and killed in self-defense without forewarning, technically speaking there should be no objection to aborting a new-born baby even once its head has emerged! Rav Hisda challenges this based on the fact that abortions were performed only in cases where the birth of the child would endanger the life of the mother. According to the Jewish tradition, an unborn baby can indeed constitute a *rodef*, pursuing after the life of the mother through the act of birth. However, both of these Rabbis already knew that it was not permitted to harm a baby once its head had emerged. Therefore, Rav Hisda challenged Rav Huna to defend his logic in the face of this clear contradiction to his original assertion.

Another added layer to this complicated objection by Rav Hisda is that the teaching he quotes to contradict Rav Huna is a more ancient rabbinic teaching than the teachings of their own contemporary generation. In the world of rabbinic disputation, the more ancient a source was, the more authoritative it was considered. Therefore, Rav Hisda subtly goaded Rav Huna by quoting a more ancient, indisputable source. Since Rav Huna would never assert a view which contradicted a venerated earlier rabbinic source, he would be forced to abandon his view. Rav Hisda therefore challenged Rav Hisda with an argument based on both logic and tradition. Undaunted by this attack, Rav Huna justified his position: "[Rav Huna replied,] 'This case [of abortion] is different [from my position] because here she [the mother giving birth] is being pursued by Heaven [God, and not the baby]!'" (Tractate

Sanhedrin 72b) Rav Huna cleverly redefined the parameters of Rav Hisda's argument in order to salvage his original opinion. Rav Huna agreed with the earlier rabbinic teaching, which supposedly contradicted him. The reason the baby can no longer be harmed is not because of the principle, "One life may not take precedence over another life." The baby is not the *rodef*, the pursuer. On the contrary, perhaps it is God's will that this mother may die in childbirth. Therefore, not only would it be futile to try to abort the baby to save the life of the mother, it would be contrary to the divine will. Thus, Rav Huna justified his initial opinion that one need not give a warning to a pursuer before resorting to deadly force, even if the pursuer is a minor.

Changing course, the Talmud then seeks to find other ancient rabbinic teachings which do not contradict Rav Huna, but may in fact support his view:

> Shall we then say that the following [teaching] supports [Rav Huna]? If a man was pursuing after his fellow to kill him, he [an observer] can say to the pursuer [in an attempt to dissuade his pursuit]: "See here, he [the pursued] is an Israelite and a member of the covenant! And the Torah has said, 'Whoever would shed the blood of a man, that man's blood shall be shed!'" (Genesis 9:6). [In other words,] The Torah allows that the blood of the pursued may be saved even through [the loss of] the blood of the pursued! (Tractate *Sanhedrin* 72b)

The point of this passage is that since this warning to a *rodef*—a pursuer after someone else with murderous intent—is so patently absurd, it would obviously have no effect on the pursued and therefore need not be issued at all. In which case, such a warning would be superfluous, so the Talmud suggests that perhaps this teaching supports Rav Huna's position that a pursuer need not be warned.

Unwilling to concede that Rav Huna was correct, other anonymous rabbis in the Talmud continue to try and find additional objections to his opinion and attempt to undermine the potentially supportive teaching above by bringing forth a similar, but contradictory teaching instead. The passage continues and quotes a seemingly exact parallel of the last pssage, which was brought to support Rav Huna:

> However, if the pursuer replied, Come and hear [an objection to Rav Huna from an ancient teaching]: If a man was pursuing after his fellow to kill him, . . . [an observer] can say to the pursuer [in an attempt to dissuade his pursuit]: "See here, . . . [the pursued] is an Israelite and a member of the covenant! And the Torah has said, 'Whoever would shed the blood of a man, that man's blood shall be shed!'" (Genesis 9:6). [In other words,] The Torah allows that the blood of the pursued may be saved even through [the loss of] the blood of the pursued! However, if the pursuer replied [to the warning], "I know that it is so"

> [accepting the warning and ceasing the pursuit] he can no longer be killed. [But if he says,] "I do so despite your warning"—he still may be killed [to save the pursued]. (Tractate *Sanhedrin* 72b)

This passage, which is an objection to Rav Huna, is nearly parallel to the one proceeding this which was used as a support of Rav Huna. The difference in this case above is that this warning issued to a *rodef* is accepted by the Rabbis as actually being efficacious! Therefore if a warning could possibly persuade a *rodef* to cease from their attack, then a pursuer must *always* be given a warning on the off-chance that it may end up saving his life and the life of the pursued. Therefore, this second teaching contradicts Rav Huna's position that a pursuer need never be warned before using deadly force against them.

Undaunted, Rav Huna responded in order to show that while this last teaching would indeed contradict his view, there were extenuating circumstances in this particular case that invalidated it. In other words, Rav Huna claimed that certain crucial details were left out which actually support his position:

> [Rav Huna replied] This teaching was referring to a case where [the observer and the pursuer] are standing on two opposite sides of a river, so that the observer cannot possibly save the life of the pursued.

> [An anonymous rabbi then asks,] "but if this is so, why does this teaching insist that the pursuer be warned [when it would *still* be ineffective in preventing the murder of the pursued]?"
>
> [Rav Huna replied,] "What can he do? [Obviously nothing! But perhaps, even after the pursuer kills his victim, it may be possible to] Bring . . . [the pursuer] before a rabbinic court of law [for a murder trial]. And [in order for a rabbinic court of law to punish the pursuer for murder,] he must have been warned [not to kill the victim in order to establish that the murder was intentional].

Rav Huna claimed that the purpose of the warning in this hypothetical situation is not to try and prevent a murder, because that would indeed be ineffective. Rather, it is to establish grounds for a possible conviction of murder in the future should the murderer ever be brought to justice. Because there are no additional objections, the Talmud clearly concludes that Rav Huna is indeed correct in asserting that in the case of a *rodef*, the would-be murderer, need not be given any warning before rescuers utilize deadly force to neutralize the attacker.

In another part of the Talmud, the Rabbis went further and insisted that there are certain situations which require us to preempt a murderer in the defense of our own life by taking the life of the would-be murderer first. The Talmud further deliberated the case of the sneaking thief and attempts to clarify the basis for which the Torah rules that there is no blood-guilt upon the homeowner who murders the thief discovered sneaking in to his home:

> Rabba said, "What is the reason for the [permission to kill the] burglar? [The answer is that] No man is able to control himself [his anger and violent protective reactions] when his money is at stake. And since the burglar knows that the homeowner will surely oppose his theft, the burglar thinks to himself, 'If he resists me, I shall kill him!' Therefore, [the Torah, anticipating the thief's murderous mindset] says, 'If a man has come to kill you, anticipate him by killing him first!'" [Tractate *Yoma* 85b]

While the Torah does not say this at all, the Rabbis assumed that this was the reasoning behind the Torah when it exculpates the homeowner from bloodguilt in the death of the thief. The thief, as a *rodef*, need not be warned before being killed—even though he has not even yet committed a crime! These talmudic conclusions are summarized and clarified by Rambam who ruled the following:

> If you warned . . . [the pursuer] . . . and yet the pursuer did not accept the warning and continued to chase after his victim; if you [can] save the pursuer

> through the loss of a limb of the pursuer—for instance if you were to shoot him with an arrow or strike him with a stone or sword and cut off his hand or break his leg or blind his eye—you should do so!
>
> But if you are not able to aim and still save the life of the pursuer except by killing the pursuer, behold [then he is one of those] whom it is permitted to kill even though they have not yet killed. [Mishneh Torah, *Hilchot Rotzeach* 1:7)

This entire discussion is predicated on the assumption that innocent bystanders will risk their lives to intervene in a potentially dangerous situation. The Torah does not take such altruism for granted. In fact, it is actually commanded in the Torah that it is prohibited for someone to stand by and witness a murder without trying to prevent it. Leviticus 19:16 states, "You shall not stand idly by the blood of your neighbor." The Talmud states this explicitly:

> Mishnah: The following [people] must be "saved" [from committing a crime] even at the cost of their lives [in order to prevent their crime]: He who pursues after his neighbor to kill him . . .
>
> Gemara (later rabbinic commentary states): Our rabbis said, "From where do we know that he who pursues his neighbor to kill him must be saved [from his crime] even at the cost of his own life? From the

verse, 'You shall not stand idly by the blood of your neighbor.'" [Tractate *Sanhedrin* 73a]

In the Christian Bible, Jesus tells a story about a Samaritan—a man from a sect antagonistic to Judaism—who helped a Jewish traveler in need. (Luke 10:29–37) This became the source of the concept of the "good Samaritan" in Western culture—that is, someone who is willing to go beyond accepted social protocol to help others in need. As wonderful as this might be, the Jewish tradition does not assume that there is an underlying streak of benevolence within human nature. In fact, God states in the Torah, "The Lord saw how great was man's wickedness on earth, and how every plan devised by his mind was nothing but evil all the time." (Genesis 6:5) Therefore, the Torah clearly defines what it expects of human beings, especially of the Jewish people. It not only allows people to defend themselves, even through the use of deadly force, but commands us to defend others in need as well.

However, the Torah also recognizes the reality of even greater violence—mass self defense in war as well as offensive warfare. Thus, the Jewish tradition also addresses how the Jewish people should conduct themselves when waging war.

5

War

War is a constant in human history. The earliest examples of writing include the annals of war, conquest, and defeat. The Hebrew Bible is also filled with tales of war. Yet, it is also the Torah that provides the first rules of warfare. Long before the modern rules of war were codified in the Geneva Conventions, the Torah provided a set of ethical principles for the Israelites to follow when they engaged in combat.

The Torah provides a myriad of laws regarding the conduct of wars (see Deuteronomy, Chapter 20). The chapter begins with God telling the Israelites that they should not fear when they take the field against their enemies for they should know that God is with them. In fact, a specially anointed priest for war shall address the troops to rally them, declaring, "Hear, O Israel! You are about to join battle with your enemy. Let not your courage falter. Do not be in fear, or in panic, or in dread of them. For it is the Lord your God who marches with you to do battle for you against your enemy, to bring you victory." (Deuteronomy 20:2–4)

This priest was to issue a call for those who were to be exempt from this draft to depart from the army. He would ask the people:

> Is there anyone who has built a new house but has not dedicated it? Let him go back to his home, lest he die in battle and another dedicate it. Is there anyone who has planted a vineyard but has never harvested it? Let him go back to his home, lest he die in battle and another harvest it. Is there anyone who has paid the bride-price for a wife [i.e. become engaged by giving a dowry but not yet consummated the marriage] but who has not yet married her? Let him go back to his home, lest he die in battle and another marry her. [Deuteronomy 20:5–7]

Because of the likelihood or at least danger of death, the Torah seems loathe to deprive certain categories of men from experiencing unique joys in their lives. In addition to exempting those men from the draft, the priest was to invite anyone who was fearful of war and whose lack of courage may lower the morale of the rest of the army to leave as well. He was to say, "Is there anyone afraid and disheartened? Let him go back to his home, lest the courage of his comrades wane like his." (Deuteronomy 20:8) The Talmud adds that although the soldiers who are frightened of warfare may be excused from participating in actual combat, they are not exempt from supplying their fellow comrades-in-arms with food and water and repairing the roads back at home. (Tractate *Sotah* 43a)

After these instructions from the priest, the Torah specifies certain tactics the Israelites were to utilize in war based on ethics. Before laying siege to a town, the Torah declares, "You shall offer it terms of peace. If it responds peaceably and lets you in, all the people present there shall serve you at forced labor. If it does not surrender to you, but would join battle with you, you shall lay siege to it. . . ." (Deuteronomy 20:10–12) The Torah then goes on to state that after capturing the city, the men should all be killed, but the women, the children, livestock, and treasures of the town may be seized as spoils of war. (Deuteronomy 20:13–14)

The Torah, however, is careful to specify that these previous laws regarding the appropriate conduct of a seige apply only to the nations which surround the promised land of Israel. As for those peoples who inhabit the land of Canaan, which God promised to the Israelites, God declares that no inhabitants should remain alive, ". . . lest they lead you into doing all the abhorrent things that they have done for their gods and you shall stand guilty before the Lord your God." (Deuteronomy 20:18) It seems that God was using the Israelites as a weapon of punishment against the Canaanite peoples for immoral religious practices. As difficult as this may be to accept, the Torah takes a profoundly harsh and unforgiving attitude towards the Canaanites. In the ideology of the Torah, however, this same theology was applied to the Israelites when they worshiped idols and were ultimately conquered and exiled from the land.

Perhaps the most fascinating aspect of these rules of war is the last part of this chapter which states,

> When in your war against a city you have to besiege it a long time in order to capture it, you must not destroy its trees, wielding the ax against them. You may eat of them, but you must not cut them down. Are trees of the field human to withdraw before you into the besieged city? Only trees that you know do not yield food may be destroyed; you may cut them down for constructing siege works against the city that is waging war on you, until it has been reduced. [Deuteronomy 20:19–20]

The Torah reveals a sense of justice even towards fruit-bearing trees because they are unable to seek refuge in a city, and therefore are left unprotected in the face of the onslaught. In addition, perhaps the Torah is concerned with the continuity of life on the land after the war. As conflicts come and go, the fruit-bearing trees must be left unmolested in order to nurture life, which will resume once peace returns.

There is an addendum to these laws of warfare

several chapters later dealing with the subject of ritual purity and impurity. The Torah commands that any male who has experienced a nocturnal emission must leave the army camp, but that towards evening he may go and immerse himself in a ritual cleansing body of water to repurify himself, and therefore re-enter the camp. (Deuteronomy 23:10–12) Many scholarly tracts have been devoted to the biblical concepts of ritual purity and pollution. Although it is an imprecise model, the closest modern analogy to this ancient system is that of electricity.

In the Torah, the Israelites were commanded to always try to maintain themselves in a ritually clean or pure state, associated with life and community. This would be like maintaining a positive charge, or having a lack of electrons, which carry a negative charge. When Israelites come into contact with certain objects or people who have somehow been associated with death, it renders them unclean or ritually polluted. Such things which exude ritual pollution—similar to an excess of negatively charged electrons—are a corpse, a dead "un-kosher" animal, and even human beings who have experienced some kind of life leak—a woman in menstruation, whose blood flow signifies a loss of potential life, or a male who has experienced a nocturnal emission, also tantamount to a loss of potential life. Once unclean or polluted, the affected person must remove themselves from possible physical contact with others until they can repair to the ritual bath—called a *mikvah*, or "pool of natural waters." Symbolizing cleansing waters, or even the amniotic waters of rebirth, the *mikvah* makes one ritually pure and clean once again. Therefore, a soldier who experienced a nocturnal emission, had to leave the camp until he could purify himself.

In addition, the Torah commands that latrines be located outside the boundaries of the military garrison. (Deuteronomy 23:13) In fact, every soldier is commanded to have a tool to dig a hole for a field toilet as part of his military issue: "With your gear you shall have a spike, and when you have squatted you shall dig a hole with it and cover up your excrement. Since the Lord your God moves about in your camp to protect you and to deliver your enemies to you, let your camp be holy; let God not find anything unseemly among you and turn away from you." (Deuteronomy 23:14–15) The Torah provides a rationale for this sanitary code—God is present in the army camp. Therefore, the army must do everything it can to create a pure and holy environment for God's presence as a means to ensure their own victory. Thus, hygienic purity is linked to ritual purity in the war camp.

Just as the Torah differentiates between the one commanded war—complete extermination of the Canaanite peoples—and wars against neighboring nations, so too does the Talmud further delineate different catagories of war. These laws of warfare are scattered throughout the Torah and the Talmud and in later rabbinic codes of law. The Rabbis divided warfare into two classes—a commanded, or obligatory war, and an optional war.

According to Rambam, a commanded war refers only to wars which God directly commanded the Israelites to wage. These wars were directed against the Canaanite nations in order to dispossess them of their land:

> When the Lord your God brings you to the land that you are about to enter and possess, and God dislodges many nations before you—the Hittites, Girgashites, Amorites, Canaanites, Perizzites, Hivites, and Jebusites, seven nations much larger than you—and the Lord your God delivers them to you and you defeat them, you must doom them to destruction: grant them no terms and give them no quarter. [Deuteronomy 7:1–2]

Another commanded war in the Torah was the war against the nation of Amalek, considered the archetypal enemy of the Jewish people:

> Remember what Amalek did to you on your journey, after you left Egypt—how undeterred by fear of God, he surprised you on the march, when you were famished and weary, and cut down all the stragglers in your rear. Therefore, when the Lord your God grants you safety from all your enemies around you, in the land that the Lord your God is giving you as a hereditary portion, you shall blot out the memory of

Amalek from under heaven. Do not forget! [Deuteronomy 25:17–19]

In addition to these two biblically commanded wars, another such commanded war is a war of self-defense. In such wars, the biblical exemptions for various soldiers as specified above are waived. The Talmud even declares that in a commanded war, everyone goes out to fight, "even a groom from under his wedding canopy and the bride from her wedding canopy." (Tractate *Sotah* 10a)

The other category of war is an optional war, such as war to expand the borders of the land of Israel, or to increase the fame and reputation of the people of Israel. Such a war can only be conducted if a Jewish king of the land of Israel secures permission of a *Sanhedrin*, a grand court consisting of seventy-one judges. As the Talmud states, "An optional war can [only] be waged by the authority of a court of seventy-one." (Tractate *Sanhedrin* 2b) An example of such wars were those waged by King David during his reign in which he conquered neighboring nations and they became part of the empire of the Israelite kingdom.

The Rabbis, based on the laws of the Torah, also legislated the disposition of war booty—such as women captured and then taken as wives (Deuteronomy 21:10 ff)—and even permitted soldiers to violate the dietary laws of *Kashrut* when engaged in a military campaign. (Tractate *Chulin* 17a) The Rabbis also relaxed several other, minor aspects of ritual law for soldiers in a war, such as being permitted to eat food without first having to ritually wash their hands, or making the special blessing over this washing. (Tractate *Eruvin* 17a)

Despite the Rabbis' legislation of warfare, their ultimate concern was that of peace. The purpose of these rules was not only to provide an ethical and moral framework within which to wage war, but also to try to vitiate the need to engage in war in the first place. Even in the midst of war, the Jewish tradition is far more concerned with how to achieve peace.

6

Peace

The fact that warfare is even regulated by the Rabbis indicates the underlying ethical approach of the Jewish tradition towards violence in general. Despite the many laws dealing with war, peace is the single most important value in Judaism. In fact, it was prohibited by the Rabbis to engage in either of the two types of warfare—a commanded war or an optional war of conquest—without first offering terms for peace. This is based on the Torah, which says: "When you approach a town to attack it, you shall offer it terms of peace [i.e. call on it to surrender]. If it responds peaceably and lets you in, all the people present there shall serve you at forced labor. If it does not surrender to you, but would join battle with you, you shall lay siege to it." (Deuteronomy 20:10–12)

Rambam added an additional term of peace which is not mentioned in the Torah: the inhabitants must agree to accept and live by the "seven commandments for the descendents of Noah." (Mishneh Torah, *Hilchot Melachim* 6:1) The Jewish tradition is predicated on the 613 commandments enumerated in the Torah. These commandments, and their rabbinic spins offs and interpretations, as well as later developments, are understood in the Jewish tradition to be incumbent upon all Jews.

However, the Rabbis of the Talmud also firmly believed that non-Jews must also adhere to certain basic moral commandments in the Torah, which they refer to as the "seven commandments for the descendents of Noah." This refers to all human beings alive today who are understood to be descendents of Noah, the patriarch of humanity who survived the biblical deluge. While Jews are also included in this category, Jews are considered primarily the descendents of Abraham, an ancestor of Noah, and obligated to observe all 613 commandments of the Torah. The seven basic commandments, which the Rabbis believed that all civilized human beings should follow are:

1. Prohibition of idolatry
2. Prohibition of blasphemy
3. Prohibition of murder
4. Prohibition of incest
5. Prohibition of theft
6. Requirement to establish courts of law
7. Prohibition against cutting off and eating the limb of an animal while still keeping the animal

alive for later consumption (as this was considered unspeakably cruel) [Exodus Rabba, 30:9 and Tractate *Sanhedrin* 59b)

The inhabitants of cities to be besieged were to be given at least two, perhaps three, chances to accept terms for surrender. One midrash (rabbinic folktale) claims that Joshua, when leading the Israelites in the conquest of the land of Israel after they had arrived at the Promised Land, sent three letters to the Canaanite peoples, each time offering them an opportunity to make peace:

> Joshua sent three letters before he entered the land: In the first he declared, "Whoever wants to flee should flee!" In the second he declared, 'Whoever wants to make peace should make peace!' In the third he declared, 'Whoever wants to wage war—let them fight!' [Mishneh Torah, *Hilchot Melachim* 6:5, based on Yerushalmi Tractate *Shevi'it* 6:1]

If the residents of a city refuse to accept terms for surrender, the Torah very clearly allows the Israelites to be quite vicious in their conduct of the war. As it says, "When the Lord your God delivers it into your hand, you shall put all its males to the sword." (Deuteronomy 20:13) However, even during the conduct of the siege, Rambam insisted that a safe passage for escape be maintained so that all who want to flee are able. Rambam wrote, "When besieging a town to capture it, do not encircle it from all four directions, rather, from only three. You should leave an avenue of escape to whoever wants to flee for their life. . . ." (Mishneh Torah, *Hilchot Melachim* 6:7)

Once the inhabitants of a city accepted these twin conditions, of surrendering and accepting the "seven commandments for the descendents of Noah," then the Torah permitted them to be put to forced labor. However, the Rabbis, like the Geneva Conventions which established rules for the treatment of prisoners of war, delineated what was acceptable forced labor for captured residents of a town. Rambam wrote, "The [captured residents] must be prepared to labor on behalf of the [conquering Jewish] king, both physically, and with their wealth. For example, this would include building walls, strengthening fortifications, and building the king's palace, and so on." (Mishneh Torah, *Hilchot Melachim* 6:1) Although the Torah, and even the additional regulations of the Rabbis, were no guarantees against abuse or deliberate misinterpretation, the cultural assumption was that captured male residents had significant value in terms of their physical service for the conquering army.

The Torah also stipulates how to treat the captured women of a city. They were not to be sexually molested but were instead considered potential brides of their captors. As the Torah states:

> When you take the field against your enemies, and the Lord your God delivers them into your power and you take some of them captive, and you see among the captives a beautiful woman and you desire her and would take her to wife, you shall bring her into your house, and she shall trim her hair, pare her nails, and discard her clothes of captivity. She shall spend a month's time in your house lamenting her father and mother; after that you may come to her and possess her, and she shall be your wife. Then, should you no longer want her, you must release her outright. You must not sell her for money; since you had your will with her, you must not enslave her. [Deuteronomy 21:10–14]

The Torah clearly recognized the inhumanity of war, yet given the brutality of the situation, attempted to humanize the conduct and treatment of prisoners as much as possible given the cultural reality of that era. Another fascinating rule of war that the Rambam included related to appropriate conduct of peace negotiations: "It is forbidden to lie in [such an offer] of a peace treaty and to deceive [the inhabitants] after you have concluded peace and they have accepted the 'seven commandments for the descendents of Noah.'" (Mishneh Torah, *Hilchot Melachim* 6:3)

Honesty is not one of the qualities that many people might associate with the conduct of war. Yet, the value of peace is so great in the Jewish tradition that once it has been achieved, even through terms of surrender, it cannot be violated or abrogated. Despite the omnipresent reality of war, the Rabbis continued to insist that peace was still the most significant value in the Jewish tradition. Many rabbis throughout rabbinic literature attest to the enduring importance of peace: "Rabban Shimon ben Gamliel said, "On three things does the world stand—on justice, on truth, and on peace." (Mishnah *Pirkei Avot* 1:18) The later Rabbis explained this early rabbinic statement to mean that, "If judgment [justice] is executed, truth is then vindicated, and peace prevails." (*Yerushalmi* Tractate *Ta'anit* 4:2) In other words, all of these three values are interconnected and dependent upon one another. In fact, the Rabbis understood their mission in the world as establishing peace in our world:

> Rabbi Elazar taught in the name of Rabbi Hanina, "[Rabbinic] scholars increase peace in the world, as it says, 'And all of your children will be learned in [the ways of] God, and great will be the peace of your children.' (Isaiah 54:13) Don't read [the Hebrew word as] 'your children' [*banayich* as it is written and implied in the Bible] rather, read it as if it said, 'your builders'" (*bonayich*). [Tractate *Berachot* 64a]

This passage is predicated on a subtle Hebrew word play. Rabbi Elazar attempted to prove that rabbinic scholars play a crucial role in creating world peace by quoting a text from the prophet Isaiah. In the verse,

Isaiah maintains that children who are knowledgeable about the Torah—i.e. rabbinic scholars—can increase peace in society. However, Rabbi Elazar asked the reader to deliberately misread one of the Hebrew words in the verse from Isaiah. In order to understand his pun, it is important to know that the Hebrew Bible in ancient times was handwritten and did not include any vowel marks to aid pronunciation. The pronunciation of words was based on context and tradition.

Therefore, it was possible to read the Hebrew words in a variety of different ways, even though there was really only one official and contextually correct way to understand it. Therefore, Rabbi Elazar suggested that instead of reading the Hebrew word as "your children," which makes sense in this context, he recommended that we interpret this Hebrew word as "your builders." He suggested this because the two words, "your children" (*banayich*) and "your builders" (*bonayich*), are nearly the exact same words in Hebrew. The only difference is in the pronunciation. Thus, Rabbi Elazar supported his statement that rabbinic scholars increase peace in the world by suggesting that the great prophet Isaiah said the same thing, namely, that those learned in the ways of God (i.e. rabbinic scholars) build and establish peace in the world.

"Rabbi Shimon bar Yochai taught, 'Great is peace because all of the other blessings are included in it, as it says, "God will grant strength to His people: God will bestow [bless] peace on His people"'" (Psalms 29:11)

(Leviticus Rabba 9:9). In this passage, Rabbi Shimon bar Yochai based his assertion of the all-inclusive nature of peace as a blessing from God on the poetic structure of biblical poetry. Poetry in the Bible is characterized by what is called "parallelism"—that is, what is said in one verse is then immediately repeated with different words in the next half of the verse. Therefore, when the Psalm says, "God will grant *strength* to His people," (emphasis added) this is parallel to the next clause, "God will bestow [or bless] *peace* on His people." Strength and peace are therefore given equal weight and, according to Rabbi Shimon bar Yochai, these gifts, which are one and the same, include all other possible gifts and blessings that God could provide the Jewish people.

Peace is indeed a great and highly-prized value, but unless it is actualized in reality and in our everyday lives, it remains only a promise. Unless enmity and hatred can be assuaged, unless the threat of violence and even war is removed, of what practical use is the glorification of peace? Perhaps the Rabbis understood this when they said, "Who is mighty? Whoever transforms his enemy into his friend." (*Avot deRebbi Natan* 23:1)

PART II

Drugs (Alcohol) in the Jewish Tradition

7

Wine in the Hebrew Bible

The production and consumption of alcohol, whether wine, beer, or other alcoholic drinks like mead, have been well-known to ancient humans for thousands of years. In fact, some of the oldest excavations in Egypt have turned up the remains of ancient breweries, and in Israel they have found pre-biblical evidence of wine production. Thus, humans have been familiar with alcohol and its effects since the dawn of civilization. Even the Psalms in the Hebrew Bible mention that "wine cheers the hearts of men" (Psalm 104:15) and that "wine makes life merry." (Ecclesiastes 10:19)

As the Bible attests, for millennia human beings have used a wide variety of stimulants, depressants, hallucinogens and other psychotropic substances—both naturally occurring and artificial. It would seem that nearly all human cultures have sought conscious escape from this world in some form or another. Each society judges these substances—either to demonize or sanctify them—in accordance with its own unique moral values.

The Hebrew Bible takes a decidedly negative attitude toward wine and by extension, toward all alcoholic drinks. Wine was considered a necessary part of life in the Ancient Near East and all of its qualities, both positive and negative, were well-known. Excessive drinking, leading to intoxication, was frowned upon. God even commanded Israelite priests to avoid drinking before engaging in their sacred duties: "And the Lord spoke to Aaron saying, 'Drink no wine or other intoxicant, you or your sons, when you enter the Tent of Meeting, that you may not die. This is a law for all time throughout the ages, for you must distinguish between the sacred and the profane. . . .'" (Leviticus 10:8–11) Because of the spiritually-sensitive function of the priests, and the ritual significance of their actions as representatives of the Israelites before God, it was considered too great a risk to allow them to imbibe before performing their sacred rites. Like airline pilots who are only prohibited from drinking before flying, the priests were simply not permitted to drink before entering the sacred Tent of Meeting. The lives of the entire community were in their hands and therefore, their judgments could not be impaired.

However, sometimes the effects of wine can be confused with those of heart-felt prayer. The high priest Eli once made this mistake when he saw Hannah in silent prayer that God would grant her a son: "Now Hannah was praying in her heart; only her lips moved, but her voice could not be heard. So Eli thought she was drunk. Eli said to her, 'How long will you make a drunken spectacle of yourself? Sober up!'" (I Samuel 1:13–14) Clearly, not only was it forbidden for the priests to drink in the tabernacle, it was also considered inappropriate for worshippers to pray while under the influence. Of course, the point of this passage is to contrast Hannah's quite sober and heart-felt petitions with Eli's inability to differentiate between true, wordless prayer and drunken mumbling. In fact, Hannah's prayers for a son were ultimately granted and her son, Samuel, eventually served Eli and became one of the greatest prophets of Israel.

Apart from these stories, the Hebrew Bible also contains many statements referring to wine and intoxication in general. The book of Proverbs is filled with such pithy statements:

> Wine is a scoffer, strong drink a roisterer;
> He who is muddled by them will not grow wise.
> [Proverbs 20:1]

> Do not be of those who guzzle wine
> Or glut themselves on meat.
> For guzzlers and gluttons will be impoverished
> And drowsing will clothe you in tatters.
> [Proverbs 23:19–21]

The book of Proverbs is a collection of aphorisms and witty, clever sayings classified as "wisdom literature." There is nothing particularly Jewish or characteristic of Israelite culture in these sayings, for wisdom literature was considered to be universal in its appeal and insights. However, these texts do express a strongly worded warning against drinking alcohol. Those who drink to excess will end up making fools of themselves, missing opportunities to grow both wiser and richer, because they only spend their money on wine.

In addition to these statements, there are many biblical characters associated with excessive drinking, none of whom were considered exemplary. Despite Noah's role as the builder of the Ark—saving his family and humanity from the biblical deluge—he was also the first drunkard of the Bible: "Noah, the tiller of the soil, was the first to plant a vineyard. He drank of the wine and became drunk, and he uncovered himself within his tent." (Genesis 9:20–7) One of Noah's sons, Ham, saw his father naked and told his two brothers, who took a cloak and entered the tent. They walked backwards so as not to embarrass their father, and themselves, and covered him up. For reasons which are not entirely clear, Noah cursed Ham but praised his other sons who covered him. Whatever the reasons were for this curse and blessing, Noah was not considered one of the most praiseworthy people by the later rabbis who commented upon this incident. Whether the Rabbis were biased or not, it is clear from a simple reading that Noah, as the first vintner, did not behave responsibly upon discovering the effects of wine.

Although Noah merely uncovered himself, other characters in the Bible behaved far worse while under the influence, especially Lot and his two daughters:

> Lot . . . and his two daughters lived in a cave. And the older one said to the younger, "Our father is old, and there is not a man on earth to consort with us in the way of all the world. Come, let us make our father drink wine, and let us lie with him, that we may maintain life through our father." That night they made their father drink wine, and the older one went in and lay with her father; he did not know when she lay down or when she rose. . . . [Genesis 19:31–33]

Following the destruction of Sodom and Gomorrah, Lot and his two daughters believed themselves to be the only surviving humans on the face of the earth. Not knowing of the entirely local nature of the destruction, they incorrectly assumed that they were responsible for repopulating the earth. Using wine, they seduced their own father and committed incest with him, eventually giving birth to nations who became enemies of the Israelite people. Whether or not this was a literary way to malign one's enemies, the use of wine in such a morally reprehensible activity casts alcohol and its effects in a poor light, associating it with sexual debauchery.

In the Hebrew Bible, wine is also associated with buffoons—characters who make foolish, self-destructive decisions. One such character is Nabal, a rich man who refused to assist the future-king David when he was on the run from King Saul, who suspected him of plotting rebellion. When David and his band of mercenaries turned to Nabal for food and shelter, he contemptuously refused them. However, Nabal's wife, Abigail, who sympathized with David, provided substantial provisions for him and his men. In explaining why her husband refused to help David, Abagain ridiculed Nabal's decision and apologized to David, saying, "Please, my Lord, pay no attention to that wretched fellow, Nabal. For he is just what his name says: his name means, 'boor' and he is indeed a boor!" (I Samuel 25:25) Abigail is referring to the fact that the name Nabal is a Hebrew word meaning a fool or buffoon. In his anger, David threatened to kill Nabal and his entire family, but Abigail assisted David without informing her husband because he was drunk. Nabal then suffered for his short-sightedness:

> When Abigail came home to Nabal, he was having a feast in his house, a feast fit for a king. Nabal was in a merry mood and very drunk, so she did not tell him anything at all until daybreak. The next morning, when Nabal had slept off the wine, his wife told him

> everything that had happened, and his courage died within him, and he became like a stone. About ten days later the Lord struck Nabal and he died. [I Samuel 25:36–38]

Although not explicitly dealing with the effects of wine, Nabal is naturally enough associated with drinking. Therefore, his foolish behavior is entirely consistent with his portrayal as a drunkard in this story. In addition to thoughtlessness, wine is also associated with letting one's guard down and even with murder. In the Hebrew Bible, Amnon, one of King David's sons, raped his half-sister, Tamar. Tamar's brother, Absalom, seeking revenge for his sister, planned Amnon's murder at an upcoming banquet: "Now Absalom gave his attendants these orders, 'Watch, and when Amnon is merry with wine and I tell you to strike down Amnon, kill him!'" (II Samuel 13:28–9) Absalom's servants carried out his orders and when Amnon was unmindful due to his drinking, he was assassinated.

A more direct connection between excessive drink and murder is the case of the rebellious son in the Torah. The Torah commands that when parents have trouble with their wayward and defiant son who does not listen to or obey them, they shall bring him to the elders of their town. There they shall publicly accuse their son of his insubordination and say, "'This son of ours is disloyal and defiant. He does not heed us. He is a glutton and a drunkard.' Thereupon the men of his town shall stone him to death." (Deuteronomy 21:20) Based on the biblical culture which frowned upon drunkeness, it is not surprising that the rebellious son was to be executed for a number of sins, especially including the flaw of being a drunkard. In all of these stories above, wine is not always the direct cause of foolish decisions or tragedy, but it is related to them often enough to lend the impression that wine was closely associated with thoughtlessness and immoral behavior in biblical Israel.

The prophets of Israel also attacked excessive drinking, for they also associated it with moral insensitivity. The prophet Isaiah accused those who drink habitually of being insensitive to God's plans in the world:

> Ah, those who chase liquor
> from early in the morning,
> and till late in the evening
> are inflamed by wine!
> Have lyre and lute,
> timbrel, flute, and wine—
> but never give a thought to the plan of the Lord
> and take no note of what He is designing.
> [Isaiah 5:11–12]

> Ah, those who are so doughty—
> as drinkers of wine,
> and so valiant—
> as mixers of drink!

> Who vindicate him who is in the wrong
> in return for a bribe,
> and withhold vindication
> from him who is in the right . . .
>
> [Isaiah 5:22–23]

This passage goes on to say that for these people, drunkards who pervert justice, are considered to have rejected God and will therefore be punished. The point Isaiah makes is that those who drink alcohol trample justice since they are blind to God's universal justice.

Clearly, the Hebrew Bible does not look favorably upon those who drink, especially to excess. Inebriation was associated with moral and sexual depravity, murder, and injustice. However, drinking wine or alcohol was never expressly prohibited for the Israelites. Only the priests were proscribed from drinking, and even then only when they were about to perform their ritual duties. The Torah is clear in its disapprobation of wine but implies that in moderation, wine may indeed have an appropriate and even sacred role in the life of the people of Israel. The Rabbis of the Talmud were well aware of the biblical view of drinking and the negative aspects of drinking wine but were far more ambivalent about the effects of alcohol.

8

The Rabbis on Wine

The basic attitude of the Rabbis of the Talmud on the consumption of alcohol was mixed. They recognized the positive, beneficial aspects of drinking, yet they also recognized its negative, debilitating effects.

The Rabbis claimed that Nadav and Abihu, the two eldest sons of Aaron, who died a strange and perplexing death (described in Leviticus 10:1–3) were struck down by God because they transgressed the prohibition against serving in the tabernacle while drunk. The Rabbis wrote:

> The sons of Aaron died only because they entered the Tent of Meeting drunk with wine. Rabbi Pinchas taught in the name of Rabbi Levi, "This may be compared to the case of a king who had a faithful attendant. When the king found him standing at tavern entrances, he cut off his head in silence [without explanation] and appointed another in his

place. We would not know why he put the first to death but for the warning he gave to second attendant in this way, 'You must not enter the doorway of taverns.' Thus we know that for such a reason he had the first put to death."

Similarly, it says, "And there came forth a fire from the Lord and devoured them, and they [Nadav and Abihu] died before the Lord." (Leviticus 10:2) But we would not know why [Nadav and Abihu] died had it not been for God's commanding Aaron [immediately after this event], "Drink no wine or other intoxicant, you or your sons, when you enter the Tent of Meeting, that you may not die." (Leviticus 10:8) [Leviticus Rabba 12:1]

The Rabbis understood drunkenness to be the reason for the death of Nadav and Abihu because of a talmudic principle of biblical exegesis called *hekesh*, or in English, "juxtaposition." The story of the mysterious death of Aaron's two sons is followed immediately by the divine injunction against drinking alcohol before entering the tabernacle. Therefore, the Rabbis drew the logical conclusion that drinking in the tabernacle must have been the sin for which Nadav and Abihu lost their lives while in sacred service.

Considering the connection between drinking alcohol and God's punishment of Nadav and Abihu, the Rabbis enacted a series of prohibitions against drinking alcohol before engaging in rabbinical and judicial functions. The first of these was: "He who has drunk one fourth [of a *log*] of wine shall not render a legal decision." (Tractate *Ketubot* 10b) A *log* was an ancient measure of volume equivalent to approximately six eggs. Therefore, the Rabbis decreed that no rabbi should be allowed to sit in judgement on any legal decision after drinking approximately one and a half egg's worth of wine. Even though this is not a lot of wine, the Rabbis were concerned about even the slightest effects the alcohol could have on matters of official judgment, especially in cases of life or death. Rabbis in ancient times did not only render religious decisions, but also served as judges in criminal cases, including cases of capital punishment. "The judges would disperse in pairs [to discuss the case overnight] and they would eat little food and would drink no wine." (Mishnah *Sanhedrin* 5:5) In discussing a case of capital punishment, the Rabbis directed that the judges presiding over such a case continue to discuss the details of the trial and evidence. However, they were not allowed to drink any wine whatsoever in case it would adversely affect their judgment in such an important matter.

Even in the world of prayer and ritual, the Rabbis were cautious about drinking alcohol. In one hyperbolic statement, the Talmud claims that "One who recites the *Amidah* [central prayer in Jewish worship] when drunk is like one who serves idols." (Tractate *Berachot* 31b)

Despite these prohibitions, the Rabbis did not excuse someone's behavior even if they happened to be intoxicated. The Rabbis held that people who are drunk were still culpable for any damages they may cause and were considered legally responsible for all of their actions while intoxicated. This is clear from the Talmud: "[A person who is] drunk—his purchases are valid and his sales are valid. If he commits a sin which is punishable by the death penalty, he is to be executed. [If he commits a sins which is punishable by] lashes, he is to be lashed. The general principle in this matter is: Behold, he is like an aware person in all of his actions." (Tractate *Arakhin* 65b) This is certainly a contrast with our society and legal system which seems to make an allowance for people who are under the influence. However, these attitudes are changing. Instead of paying meager fines, judges have begun to impose severe sentences on people who are convicted of committing serious damage, even manslaughter, while driving under the influence. Perhaps our society is adopting the same underlying principle which is evident in this passage above: whenever we choose to drink, we do so in our capacity as human beings created with free will. Despite the effects of what we choose to consume, we are still ultimately responsible for all of our actions, having had the freedom to choose to drink in the first place. When we act foolishly or dangerously as a result of having chosen to drink, then we alone are responsible for our actions and must live with the consequences.

The Rabbis, of course, recognized the physiological effects of alcohol on people. In fact, the Rabbis coined a number of clever Hebrew sayings that indicate a realistic, albeit negative, attitude toward the socially destructive effects of intoxication: " 'Wine' is equivalent [in numerical value] to the number seventy. 'Secret' is also equivalent [in numerical value] to the number seventy. [Therefore,] when wine enters, secrets exit." (Tractate *Eruvin* 65a) This observation is based on the fact that all Hebrew letters have numerical values, because they were—and to some extent still are—used as numbers in Hebrew literature. The Rabbis took advantage of this in order to generate greater meaning and connections between different words and concepts. This practice of reading Hebrew words based on their numerical value, and then connecting them with other, dissimilar words within the same numerical value, is called *gematria*—derived from a Greek word which is the origin of our English word geometry. Because the Hebrew words "wine" and "secret" have the same numerical value, the Rabbis drew the obvious conclusion that when wine goes into a person, it loosens their tongue and sense of social propriety. Therefore, their secrets will come out.

Another saying reads: "Much wine—[it will] end up that he forgets his 248 limbs." (Leviticus Rabbah 12:5) This saying is based on the fact that when a person drinks a lot of alcohol, not only do they lose control of the things they say, but they also lose control of the rest of their body. The Rabbis believed that the human body is composed of 248 parts—including bones, muscles, limbs, and sinews—therefore, a person will lose complete control of his or her body if they drink enough.

This is part of a larger rabbinic idea that the Torah consists of 613 commandments. Although later rabbis—such as Rabbi Moses Maimonides—did count and enumerate them, the Rabbis of the Talmud offered no lists to substantiate their total. The Rabbis also held that 365 of these commandments were negative commandments—that is, prohibitions such as "do not murder," and "do not steal"—and the remaining 248 were positive commandments enjoining the Israelites to do certain actions—such as "remember the Sabbath," and "love your neighbor as yourself." The Rabbis explained that the 365 negative commandments corresponded to the 365 days of the solar year. Therefore, there is a symbolic safety net of injunctions and prohibitions which keep a person from transgressing God's will every day of every year. Similarly, every part of every person's body has a positive commandment corresponding to it, so that a person can fulfill God's will with all parts of their entire body.

However, when a person drinks too much, he or she loses control of the 248 parts of his or her body; one slurs speech, has trouble coordinating hands and feet, and may end up stumbling around on his or her legs. The deeper implication of this saying is that when a person is drunk, one is unable to fulfill God's will as represented by the 248 positive commandments of the Torah. Another saying reads: "Rabbi Illai said, 'Through three things a person is known—through his cup, his pocket, and his anger.'" (Tractate *Eruvin* 65b) This observation is obscure in English translation, but is rather delightful in the original Hebrew. Rabbi Illai coined an alliterative aphorism that can be grasped through transliteration. In Hebrew, "his cup, his pocket, and his anger" read like this, *b'ko-so, u've'kee-so u've'kah-so*, which sounds rather like a sentence from a Dr. Seuss book.

Such a memorable line also makes considerable sense. Rabbi Illai observed that it is possible to know the true essence of a person through "his cup"—that is, how he or she behaves after drinking alcohol. Since alcohol has the tendency to put to sleep the outermost layers of the brain, which control our superficial, social behavior, people tend to act in ways that reveal the true essence of who they are. It is also possible to know the true essence of a person through "his pocket"—that is, how a person spends his money, whether on prudent purchases or investments, or frivolous, insubstantial leisure activities and toys. And finally, it is possible to know the true essence of a person through "his anger"—that is, though how he behaves when he loses his emotional control. Does he rage and yell or curse? Or does he manage to maintain his appropriate speech and behavior despite his anger? Rabbi Illai noted that how one behaves while under the influence of alcohol can sometimes reveal the deeper side of his personality.

Rambam also disapproved of drinking excessively, especially in regard to rabbis. He wrote:

> All who drink to the point of drunkenness sin and are disgusting and lose their wisdom. And if they [meaning in this case, rabbis] become drunk before common people, behold, they have desecrated the name of God. And it is forbidden to drink wine in the afternoon, even just a little bit, except if it was in the regular course of eating and drinking. [Mishneh Torah, *Deot* 5:3]

But perhaps the clearest indication of the Rabbinic attitude towards drinking alcohol is expressed in a midrash which describes how Noah came to plant the first vineyard. The Torah portrays Noah as the father of all viticulture; he is the first person to plant a vineyard, produce wine, and get drunk. (Genesis 9:20–21) The Rabbis imaginatively portrayed this event:

> When Noah came to plant a vineyard, the Satan [in Hebrew it literally means, "the adversary"] came and stood before him and said, "What are you planting and what is the value of its fruit?" Noah said, "A

> vineyard, and its fruit is sweet, both dry and wet. And it is possible to make wine from it which gladdens the heart, as it says, 'Wine gladdens the hearts of men.'" (Psalms 104:15) The Satan said, "Come, let us make a partnership over this vineyard." Noah said, "Let us do so then."
>
> What did the Satan do? He brought a lamb and slaughtered it under the vine. Afterwards, he brought a lion and slaughtered it under the vine. Afterwards, he brought a pig and slaughtered it under the vine. And afterwards, he brought a monkey and slaughtered in under the vine, and their blood watered the vineyard.
>
> This is a hint indicating that at first when a man drinks wine, he is simple like a lamb who does not know anything, like a ewe before its shearing. When he drinks more, he becomes mighty, like a lion and says, "There is no one like me in the world." When he drinks even more, he becomes like a pig that soils itself in its own urine and excrement. When he becomes thoroughly drunk, he becomes like a monkey that dances and plays and brings all manner of filth out of its mouth and is not aware of what he is doing. And all of this happened to Noah the "righteous." [Tanchuma Genesis, Parasha 13]

This midrash presents a realistic assessment of the effects of drinking on people, noting the various stages of inebriation. While being tipsy and somewhat affected by alcohol seems to be innocuous, the more one drinks, the more odious and disgusting he becomes until by the Rabbis' comparison, he is equivalent to a pig, wallowing in its own filth. This is the epitome of an unkosher comparison. Such a description may seem to be a rather accurate and even unbiased portrayal of the effects of alcohol, except that the presence of the Satan lends a distinctly negative spin to this story.

Because we live in a predominantly Christian culture, many of our associations with Satan are naturally affected by Christian theology. In popular Christian understanding, Satan is a fallen angel, a thoroughly evil, demonistic character associated with absolute evil. However, the Rabbis saw Satan in very different terms. In fact, the word *Satan* is a Hebrew word which simply means "adversary." Satan is almost always referred to in rabbinic literature as "the" Satan, indicating the role and not the character. This is because in the rabbinic conception of the universe, the Rabbis imagined God presiding over a heavenly court sitting in on-going judgment over all individuals and nations of the world. The Rabbis simply projected their experience and familiarity with courtroom matters onto God's heavenly jurisdiction.

The Rabbis portrayed God as a judge surrounded by a retinue of angelic attorneys. Some of these heavenly counselors argue on behalf of humans and their specific nations, while others argue against them and urge

God to impose punishments. Every nation on earth had its own defense attorney as well as its own prosecutor. The Satan was simply the title of the angel who was assigned to argue against the merits of the people of Israel. In other words, he was the special prosecutor who investigated and brought to light all negative evidence which might have inclined God to rule against the Jewish people and impose suffering and punishment upon them. The Satan even seems to have the freedom to act as an agent provocateur as well, engaging in tricks and deceit in order to incriminate the Jewish people. Therefore, the Satan was a figure of danger in the Jewish tradition but by no means the incarnation of pure evil.

However, it is significant and quite telling that the Satan is present when Noah plants his first vineyard. While alcohol is not exactly the drink of the devil, it is interesting to note that the Rabbis clearly felt that drinking alcohol was an activity fraught with hazard. Yet, this did not lead the Rabbis to prohibit drinking wine. In fact, despite this fairly negative background, the Rabbis were quite willing to acknowledge and even extol the value of drinking wine.

9

The Lighter Side of Wine

Jews have a special connection to alcohol, especially wine, because this is the preferred drink for *kiddush*. *Kiddush*, which literally means "sanctification," is the special set of blessings recited over a cup of wine on *Shabbat* and festivals. Although *kiddush* can also be made using grape juice wine is preferred precisely because of its alcoholic content. This is derived from the Talmud where the Rabbis discussed whether the four cups of wine one drinks at the Passover seder may be diluted with water, to possibly eliminate the taste of alcohol in the wine. "Raba said, 'This person may have fulfilled his duty [i.e. religious obligation] for drinking [the four cups] of wine [at the Passover seder] but he has not fulfilled his duty of [drinking wine with an alcoholic taste as a symbol of] freedom.'" (Tractate *Pesachim* 108b) What this means is that wine is supposed to have a taste of alcohol, as a symbol of the freedom that the Israelites experienced when they left Egypt, and which we, as modern Jews, continue to celebrate each year at Passover. Perhaps wine, and its alcoholic taste, were also preferred by the Rabbis in the Talmud because of the intoxicating effect that helps people feel liberated from their everyday cares and worries. Despite this passage, later rabbis ruled that grape juice can also be used if someone is unable to drink wine for health reasons, or simply does not prefer the taste of wine.

Wine is also the symbol of freedom because it was an expensive drink in ancient times and as such, could only be afforded by free people, not slaves. It was the drink of nobility and the wealthy. In addition, because the Torah commands us to rejoice on *Shabbat* and the holidays, and because one of the effects of drinking wine is relaxation and feeling good, even happy, what better way to fulfill this commandment than through wine? When people drink too much, however, they do not feel so good. Therefore, Jews were encouraged to drink only enough to help them feel a little happier on *Shabbat* and the holidays. Whatever the reasons might be, the Rabbis insisted that all religious celebrations include the sanctification over wine.

Another reason that wine is the preferred beverage for making *kiddush* for *Shabbat* and festivals is that wine is made from grapes, and the Torah (Deuteronomy 9:9) says that grapes are one of the seven native plants of the land of Israel. Therefore, Jews drink wine for *kiddush* to remind us of our ancestral homeland, the land of Israel, and to help us continue to feel connected to the Promised Land. Although grapes grow in many different places all over the world, grapes remind Jews of the Holy Land.

Despite the negative—and even critical examples—of how the Rabbis viewed drinking wine and alcohol, rabbinic literature is replete with many passages extolling the virtues of wine and its benefits. For example, in one passage the Rabbis claimed that "people do not sing except because of wine." (Tractate *Berachot* 35a) In addition, the Rabbis hint that: "[What was] the tree from which the first man [Adam] ate? Rabbi Meir says it was a grapevine, for there is nothing which brings merriment to a man more than wine." (Tractate *Berachot* 40a) While popular culture seems to imagine that the fruit from the forbidden tree of the knowledge of Good and Evil was an apple, the Torah itself does not specify this. It merely refers to it as generic fruit. (Genesis 2:16–17 and 3:2) The Rabbis discussed what the fruit might have been, and Rabbi Meir suggested that perhaps the fruit was grapes from a grapevine. He even justified his answer by asserting that no other fruit could have possibly brought such joy and insight to the first man and woman in the Garden of Eden than grapes. His answer ignores the labor and skill involved in wine making. However, it is a tantalizing suggestion that no other fruit, or its manufactured product, could have had such a profound effect on human beings.

It is also interesting to note that Rabbi Meir suggests the grapevine not to disparage or attack this fruit, but rather to praise it and its qualities. Far from being a fruit filled with ominous consequences, Rabbi Meir praised the grape—and by extension, wine—precisely for its ability to bring joy to people. And perhaps he was also suggesting that rather than being a sin, it was a great benefit to human culture to learn of grapevines and wine making. In fact, the Rabbis ridiculed people who abstained from drinking wine, as demonstrated in this passage from the Talmud:

> When the Second Temple was destroyed, separatists multiplied among the people who did not eat meat or drink wine. Rabbi Joshua said to them, "My children, why do you not eat meat or drink wine?" They replied, "Shall we eat meat which used to be offered on the altar which now is no more? Shall we drink wine which used to be offered on the altar which now is no more?" He said to them, "If so, bread should also not be eaten for the meal offerings are no more. [Similarly, can] fruit be eaten? Fruit should also not be eaten because the First Fruits [offering] is no more. [Similarly, can] water be drunk? Water should also not be drunk because the water libations are no more!" [The separatists] were silent. [Tractate *Bava Batra* 60b]

This passage provides a fascinating insight into Jewish society following the destruction of the Second Temple by the Romans in 70 C.E. Apparently there were groups of mourners, called "separatists" here, who were so aggrieved that they voluntarily abstained from meat and wine, former sacrifices, and offerings on the altar of the Temple, because it reminded them of their loss. Rabbi Joshua attacked their asceticism and aggressively argued against their practice, logically demonstrating its absurdity. Clearly the rabbis at that time did not want to over-emphasize the loss of the Temple and therefore encouraged people to embrace their new life devoid of the sacrificial cult in Jerusalem. And this embrace of life included drinking wine, a symbol of joy and gladness.

The Rabbis further advocated a joyous life, especially in the service of religious festivals, in their following interpretation of one of the verses in the Torah: "A man is obligated to rejoice his children and entire household on the pilgrimage festivals, as it says, 'And you shall rejoice in your festivals.' (Deuteronomy 16:14) And with what does a person rejoice? With wine!" (Tractate *Pesachim* 109a) Not only is wine helpful in achieving joy on the holiday, the Rabbis taught that one was *obligated* to drink wine on festivals, and that this is the appropriate means by which to generate gladness and exultation. Therefore, the Rabbis were able to claim that the Torah commands the Jewish people to drink wine on festivals.

The last and most fascinating example of how highly the Rabbis esteemed drinking wine is found in regard to the customs of a nazarite. Described in the Torah (Numbers, Chapter 6), the nazarite was both a temporary and voluntary Jewish ascetic—that is, someone who would voluntarily take vows to abstain from certain activities. A nazarite could be any person who swore to temporarily refrain from cutting their hair, coming into contact with the dead, and drinking wine. People would become nazarites in order to achieve a high degree of holiness and sanctity, either in gratitude for surviving some trying event or to fulfill a promise made in a time of hardship. Upon the conclusion of their temporary period as a nazarite, according to the Torah, the former nazarite would bring a sin offering to the Temple in Jerusalem. However, the Rabbis were perplexed as to why someone who had completed their nazarite status had to bring a sin offering? The Talmud explains: "[A nazirite who completes his nazarite period] must bring a sin offering. And how has he sinned? Because he caused pain to himself by abstaining from wine!" (Tractate *Nedarim* 10a) In a radical assertion of the value and importance of drinking wine, the Rabbis claimed that the asceticism so prized by the nazarite—specifically, abstaining from wine—was itself the very sin which must be atoned for through animal sacrifice. Despite their ambivalence about wine, the Rabbis were clear in their desire to ensure that wine should always be a part of Jewish life, and life in general.

10

The Problem with Purim

Given both the positive and negative attitudes of the Rabbis toward wine, they confronted a challenging situation with the minor Jewish festival of Purim. Falling in the late winter each year, Purim celebrates the events recorded in the biblical book of Esther, which recounts how Esther and Mordecai, the central Jewish figures, managed to triumph over the evil plans of one of the Persian king's closest advisors, the Jew-hating Haman. Over the years, the celebration of Purim—even in talmudic times—included drinking much alcohol. The tradition emerged that not only should one drink alcohol on Purim, but should drink to the point of getting drunk!

The central passage that presents this unusual law appears in the talmudic tractate dealing with the festival of Purim, which is itself embedded in an unusual story:

> Rava said, "Everyone is obligated to become drunk on Purim until he can no longer distinguish between 'cursed be Haman' and 'blessed be Mordecai.'"
>
> Rabba and Rav Zeira once threw the Purim feast together. They become so drunk that Rabba went and cut Rav Zeira's throat [killing him!] The next day, Rabba prayed [to God for mercy] and resurrected him. The following year, Rabbah said to him, "Will you come and make the Purim feast together again?" [Rav Zeira] replied, "A miracle may not happen every time!" [Tractate *Megillah* 7b]

This fascinating passage begins with the unusual law in the Jewish tradition that everyone must get drunk on Purim. They must get so drunk, in fact, that they can no longer tell the difference between the two phrases, "cursed be Haman" and "blessed be Mordecai." This law is referred to by its Hebrew phrase, *ad d'lo yada*, which means "until he does not know." It is unclear whether the strange and violent story that follows is intended to emphasize the observance of this law of Purim drinking or in fact, to show the opposite.

Although the talmudic rabbis did not deal with this passage any further, later rabbis were greatly troubled by this dictum to get drunk on Purim and interpreted it in different ways. Many later rabbis were so uncomfortable with the law of *ad d'lo yada* that they resorted to unique and clever ways to reinterpret it so as to completely disregard its original intent, while other rabbis were content to advocate the spirit of drunken abandon conveyed by the original talmudic passage.

Rabbi Joseph Karo, the author of the *Shulchan Aruch*, apparently had no qualms whatsoever with simply quoting Rava's dictum from the Talmud that "everyone is obligated to become drunk on Purim until he can no longer distinguish between 'cursed be Haman' and 'blessed be Mordecai.'" (*Shulchan Aruch*, Orach Hayyim 695:2) Rabbi Karo apparently understood Rava's statement to be literal and sufficiently obvious to warrant no further comment. Namely, one should get so drunk on Purim so as to literally lose the mental capacity to distinguish between the two statements, one cursing Haman and the other blessing Mordecai.

However, the often-times anonymous authors of the *Tosafot*, a medieval commentary on the Talmud, believed that the unusual phrases, "cursed by Haman" and "blessed be Mordecai," were not as simple as they seemed. In his commentary to the talmudic passage above, the author of this particular commentary supplied what he believed was a more complete version of Rava's statement—that is, a person should get so drunk so that he: "can no longer distinguish between 'cursed be Haman' and 'blessed be Mordecai,' 'cursed be Zeresh' and 'blessed be Esther,' 'cursed be all evil doers' and 'blessed be all the Jews.'" (Tractate *Megillah* 7b, opening phrase: *de'lo yada*) Perhaps the author of this *Tosafot* commentary is suggesting that these phrases refer to a complicated religious poem or song that was traditionally sung after reading the book of Esther on the festival of Purim. In other words, when Rava says to become so drunk one cannot distinguish between cursing Haman and blessing Mordecai, perhaps the test of drunkenness was to recite this long religious song to determine whether one could still recite it correctly. If this is so, then it may be that one did not have to drink so much in order to fail this sobriety test. A superficial reading of the Talmud would indicate that someone would have to drink a prodigious amount in order to lose their capacity to differentiate between simply cursing Haman and blessing Mordecai. However, if the actual test was to recite a long, complicated song, then it may have been far easier to achieve this goal by drinking much less alcohol. Either the author of the *Tosafot* simply wanted to clarify the nature of this sobriety test in the Talmud, or he was weighing in with his own opinion as to how much alcohol it is proper to drink on Purim.

This interpretation of the *Tosafot* was supported by Rabbi Abraham ben Isaac, author of the *Sefer HaEshkol*. Rabbi Abraham ben Isaac wrote: "The ancients had a song, and at the completion of the verse, said one time: 'blessed be Mordecai' and once, 'cursed be Haman.' One time, 'blessed be Esther' and once 'cursed be Zeresh.' And anyone whose mind was not completely clear could easily confuse the verses." (Quoted in the *Beit Yosef, Orach Hayyim* 695) Even the slightest amount of drink might easily cause one to stumble over the recitation of these verses or inadvertently confuse them, thus fulfilling the talmudic dictum of becoming so drunk that one can no longer differentiate between the blessing of Mordecai and the curse of Haman.

Rabbi Moses Maimonides, however, takes an entirely different approach to dealing with Rava's obligation. Rambam was uncomfortable with endorsing a law that obligated people to get drunk. Therefore, he found an ingenious way around this requirement: "How does one fulfill the obligation of this [Purim] feast? One eats meat and prepares a beautiful meal as best he can. And he drinks wine until he becomes drunk and falls asleep in his drunkenness." (Mishneh Torah, *Hilchot Megillah* 2:15) Rather than having to actually get drunk, Rambam suggests that it is sufficient to drink enough wine so that one merely becomes sleepy. Rabbi Moses Isserles, a later rabbi, noted that once one drinks and falls asleep, he can obviously no longer distinguish between, "cursed be Haman" and "blessed be Mordecai." (*Shulchan Aruch*, Orach Hayyim 695) In addition, Rabbi Isserles extended Rambam's approach by stating that one does not need to actually drink to the point of drunkenness. Rather, one need only drink a little more than he is accustomed, and then fall asleep.

Rabbi Ephraim, who lived in North Africa a millennium ago, provided the most limiting interpretation of Rava's obligation to get drunk on Purim by actually rejecting it. He wrote:

> Since the story is brought—"Rabbah went and cut Rav Zeira's throat because they were drunk . . ." and "The next year when he said to him, 'Let us have the Purim [feast] together,' and Rav Zeira responded, 'a miracle may not happen every time,'—it follows that this statement [that one should become drunk on Purim] of Rabba is rejected! And it is correct that this should be so. [Quoted by Rabbi Avraham ben Isaac in the *Sefer HaEshkol*, Hilchot Hanukkah and Purim, Chapter 8]

First, it must be pointed out that Rabbi Ephraim seems to think that Rabbah was the Rabbi who made the initial statement in the talmudic passage about the obligation to drink. However, in our Talmud, this statement is attributed to a different Rabbi named Rava. Therefore, it can be argued that because the names are so similar in Hebrew—Rava and Rabba only differ by one Hebrew letter—that Rabbi Ephraim's manuscript copy of the Talmud might have had Rabba's name in both parts of this talmudic passage.

If this is the case, then Rabbi Ephraim's opinion is that the Talmud deliberately placed the story of Rabba's murderous drunken stupor immediately after what he believed to be Rabba's statement (regarding the obligation to get drunk on Purim) in order to negate his original dictum. In other words, Rabba's actions are recounted by the Talmud in order to disprove his originally stated obligation of getting drunk, in order to demonstrate that it should not be followed. The later editors of the Talmud may have felt that it was important to preserve the opinion that everyone must get drunk on Purim even if they did not agree with it. Therefore, these later editors deliberately juxtaposed the story about Rabbah's irresponsible drunken carousing to annul this initial opinion.

Even if there was no mix-up in Rabbi Ephraim's copy of the Talmud between the two names of Rabba and Rava, Rabbi Yoel Sirkes, who lived in Poland in the 1600s, found this interpretation valid when he wrote: "And it appears that for this reason the redactor of the Talmud arranged this story of Rabba and Rav Zeira after the statement of Rava [precisely in order to show that] this statement of Rava was the law, but that it should be cancelled." (*Beit Hadash* Commentary to *Shulchan Aruch*, Orach Hayyim 695) In other words, this statement of Rava that everyone is supposed to become drunk on Purim was presented only so that it should be cancelled. Now we have come full circle, from accepting Rava's statement—"Everyone is obligated to become drunk on Purim until he can no longer distinguish between 'cursed be Haman' and 'blessed be Mordecai.'"—at face value to using the very same talmudic passage to nullify the impact of this statement.

There are obviously many different ways to deal with the problematic aspects of Rava's dictum to drink to the point of drunkenness on Purim. However, as is obvious from many different rabbis, an obligation to get drunk was not morally acceptable to many in the Jewish tradition. Therefore, they attempted to moderate or even eliminate this so-called obligation.

11

Caring for Our Bodies

Having considered the various traditional responses to drinking and intoxication, it is equally important to understand the value that the Jewish tradition places on maintaining good health. It is naive to consider the laws and ancient sources about drinking without considering the impact such practices have on our health.

The obvious and most important point to keep in mind is the conclusion of modern medical science that the prolonged use or abuse of alcohol—or any intoxicating drug—will ultimately prove to be harmful to our health, whether in the short or long term. The Jewish tradition has much advice to offer in this area as well, namely, concerning the maintenance of good health.

In the Torah, God tells each Israelite "take the utmost care and watch yourself scrupulously" (Deuteronomy 4:9), warning the Israelites to be careful in the observance of God's laws. However, Rambam, basing himself on the Talmud, deliberately misread this verse to refer to one's health. A physician by trade, Rambam was particularly interested in how the Jewish tradition and health intersected: "Every obstacle that presents a potential mortal danger to someone, it is a commandment to remove it and to guard one's self from and be very, very careful. As it says in the Torah, 'take the utmost care and watch yourself scrupulously.'" (Mishneh Torah, *Hilchot Rotzeach*, 11:4) Rambam made this connection because the Hebrew phrase "watch yourself carefully" can be translated as "guard your life." Therefore, it is not too great a misreading of the original verse to derive this meaning. In fact, Rambam expanded on this principle when he wrote: "Since keeping one's body healthy and whole is the path of God, for it is not possible to know anything of God or understand the Creator when one is sick, a person must distance themselves from things which destroy their body and conduct themselves in ways which will make it healthy and strong." (Mishneh Torah, *Deot* 4:1)

In order to safeguard one's health, the Rabbis of the Talmud enjoined scholars of Torah from living in any place where they could not assure their physical well-being: "A scholar [and by extension any person] should not live in a city that does not have the following things: . . . public baths, a doctor. . . ." (Tractate *Sanhedrin* 17b)

Anyone can live wherever he or she may choose,

however, the Rabbis were concerned about the health and well-being of their fellow scholars and cautioned them against residing in a city that did not have adequate medical facilities. The Rabbis also considered public baths to be an important institution in the maintenance of one's health and hygiene. "When the Torah says, 'sanctify yourselves before God,' [from Leviticus 11:44, the Rabbis explained that this means we should] wash our hands before a meal, [and the verse] 'And be holy' [also from Leviticus 11:44, means that we should] wash our hands after a meal." (Tractate *Brachot* 53b)

This explanation is actually referring to the rabbinically ordained practice of ritually purifying one's self before and after eating a meal, and the recitation of certain blessings to accompany the washing of one's hands. However, the Rabbis considered keeping one's entire body clean to be not only pleasurable but also a religious obligation.

> Once, when Hillel the Elder concluded a lesson, he walked with his students and they said to him, "Where are you going?" He replied, "I am going to do a mitzvah [commandment]." They said, "Which mitzvah?" He replied, "Bathing in the bathhouse!" They said, "Is this really a mitzvah?!" He replied, "Yes! If the statues of the kings erected at theaters and circuses are scoured and washed by a man who is appointed to look after them, and thereby earns his

> living . . . how much the more so should I, who have been created in the image of God [also be performing a mitzvah by cleaning my own body]?! As it says, "In the image of God He created man." (Genesis 1:27) [Leviticus Rabba 34:3]

In this wonderful analogy, Hillel explained to his students that if it is proper to clean inanimate statues of the Roman emperors, how much more elevated and holy should it be for us, as human beings created in the image of God, to clean our own bodies!

Perhaps the most relevant principle from these sources was expressed by Rambam: "It is forbidden for a person to injure themselves or others." (Mishneh Torah, *Hilchot Hovel,* 5:1) Even though as human beings we are created with free will, and therefore, the power to use and abuse alcohol and other mind-altering substances, this does not mean that we should. In fact, it is clear from the standpoint of the Jewish tradition that we should not harm our bodies or our health in any way. However, given the assertion of the Jewish tradition that we are all created with free will, we can only hope that through education and the concern and support of other people, everyone will indeed make healthy choices in their lives.

PART III

Sex in the Jewish Tradition

12

Morality and Sexuality

Rav Kahana once hid under the bed of Rav [a famous talmudic rabbi referred to simply as "Rav"] while he made love to his wife. He heard how he spoke and played and fulfilled his needs. [Rav Kahana] said, "He is like a hungry lion who has not eaten!" [Rav] called out, "Kahana?—get out! This is not appropriate! He replied, "But this is Torah and I must learn!"

(*Tractate Berachot* 62a)

Many people are surprised to learn that sex is a matter of Torah. As one of the most ecstatic and divine of all human activities, it also carries the potential for the grossest abuses and most destructive traumas. Therefore, sexuality is a topic of legitimate study in the Jewish tradition. Although the talmudic sage Rav was upset to discover his student Rav Kahana hiding under his bed while he made love to his wife, he did not disagree with Rav Kahana's defense that "this is Torah and I must learn!" Not only was Rav a teacher of Torah, but he was a teacher of lovemaking as well!

The Torah sees sex as a good, divine activity but acknowledges that it carries the potential for misuse. That is why decisions about sex must be carefully considered and why the Jewish tradition seeks to regulate sexual activity and channel it towards holy purposes. Although rarely explicit, the Torah deals with sexuality sometimes directly and sometimes as part of other narratives. However, its strong moral messages can be discerned through careful reading and analysis.

In the passage relating to the the creation of the first humans, God initially created a male, but then "The Lord God said, 'It is not good for the man to be alone. I will make a fitting helper for him.'" (Genesis 2:18) Although it should be noted that in the first chapter of Genesis, the Torah does state that God "created man in His image, in the image of God He created him; male and female He created them." (Genesis 1:27) This verse clearly indicates that God created male and female at the same time, whereas the second chapter of Genesis relates the familiar story of the creation of Adam first and then Eve. Some rabbis claimed that these are two completely separate stories of the creation of the first humans, while other rabbis claimed that these are actually two different versions of the same, initial story of the creation of humanity. According to this latter understanding, Chapter One of Genesis provides the overview of the creation of the first humans but, chapter two provides the details. In either case, the point of both verses is clear: It is part of God's divine plan that males and females should be paired with one another. The implication that this pairing should include sexual relations is clear from another verse where Adam, the first male, expresses his excitement upon meeting Eve, his mate: "Then the man said, 'This one at last is bone of my bones and flesh of my flesh. This one shall be called Woman, for from man she was taken.' Hence, a man leaves his father and mother and clings to his wife, so that they become one flesh." (Genesis 2:23–24) Adam immediately recognizes that Eve is a part of him, either literally or figuratively, and he names her. In Hebrew, the word for man is *ish* and the word for woman is *ishah*, which can be understood to mean "from man." Our English words preserve this connection; the word *woman* includes the word *man*. Then the Torah declares that because Eve was created from Adam's flesh, it is the natural way of the universe that a man should cling or cleave to his wife so that they become one flesh once again. In other words, through sexual union, a man and woman recapitulate this initial corporeal unity as represented through the story of Adam and Eve. One of the first activities that Adam and Eve engage in is procreation, giving birth to Cain and Abel, and later, to other children.

Despite this initial, positive and even divine endorsement of procreative sexuality, the potential for abuse soon begins to manifest itself. When three men, divine messengers or angels, visit Lot in Sodom, the local townspeople gather about Lot's house. "They shouted to Lot and said to him, 'Where are the men who came to you tonight? Bring them out to us, that we may "know" them.'" (Genesis 19:4) The Hebrew Bible prefers to use the verb *to know* as a euphemism for sexual union, understanding the term to refer to intimate knowledge of someone else. In this case, Lot's neighbors not only violate the norms of hospitality, but demand to homosexually rape Lot's guests.

Lot, however, appears to fare no better than his neighbors, for in a vain attempt to appease the mob, he offers his daughters in the place of his guests: "'Look, I have two daughters who have not known a man. Let me bring them out to you, and you may do to them as you please; but do not do anything to these men, since they have come under the shelter of my roof.'" (Genesis 19:8) Lot's sense of decency seems to be no better than that of his fellow inhabitants of Sodom; he deemed it appropriate to hand over his virgin daughters for gang rape, rather than compromise his guests. Yet, even that offer is rejected and ultimately, Lot's guests effect their own rescue through divine means. The Torah subtly communicates its abhorrence of both homosexual and heterosexual rape by condemning Sodom's inhabitants to divine destruction.

Lot's daughters must have been morally desensitized or traumatized by their upbringing in Sodom, for the next time they appear in the Torah's narrative, they are committing incest with their father, naively believing themselves to be the last humans on earth. (Genesis 19:30–37) The Torah reveals its disgust with their actions by naming the incestuous offspring after the future enemies of the people of Israel.

Even in these early stories, the Torah reveals a clear moral disgust with rape. Later, another incident of rape results in harsh punishment when Dina, Jacob's only daughter, is raped by Shechem, one of the Canaanite inhabitants of the land. Despite his protestations of love and the willingness of his people to undergo circumcision in order to marry into Jacob's clan, two of Jacob's sons take matters into their own hands: "On the third day, when they were in pain, Shimon and Levi, two of Jacob's sons, brothers of Dina, took each his sword and came upon the city unmolested, and slew all the males." (Genesis 34:25) Despite the fact that Jacob did not approve of the violence of his two sons, this incident nonetheless communicates the Torah's revulsion with rape. Whether due to ancient concepts of purity and pollution, social and moral boundaries, or an understanding of the natural order of the world, the Torah establishes clear parameters for sexuality. Each of the morally proscribed and problematic sexual unions underscore the Torah's moral understanding of the realm of sexuality.

The Rabbis understood sexuality as a form of behavior particularly subject to a person's *yetzer ha-rah.* Literally, this means "evil inclination." Just as popular cartoons portray characters faced with moral choices with a little angel on one shoulder and a little devil on the other, the Rabbis of the Talmud portrayed human beings as being equally drawn between their good and evil inclinations as part of our original nature. The Rabbis imagined that we are constantly attracted, back and forth, between following *yezter ha-rah,* the evil inclination, and *yetzer ha-tov,* the good inclination. In fact, the Rabbis claimed that no less than God created humans this way: "Rav Nahman bar Rav Hisda taught, 'Why was it written, "And the Lord God created the man" (Genesis 2:7) using two *yods* [Hebrew letters]? To indicate that man was created with two impulses—the good impulse and the evil impulse.'" (Tractate *Berachot* 61a) The Rabbis were meticulous readers of the Torah and every unusual grammatical usage elicited a wide range of creative interpretations. In this case, the Hebrew word *to create* used in the verse where God creates the first man, is spelled in an unusual fashion, including two Hebrew letter *yods* where only one is needed. To the Rabbis, this was not an inadvertent misspelling, but rather, a hint of the divine plan for human beings. Because the Hebrew word *yetzer,* meaning "inclination," begins with a single *yod,* the Rabbis surmised that the presence of these two *yods* in *create* in the context of creating the first man meant that Adam was created with both a *yod* for his *yetzer ha-rah* and a *yod* for his *yetzer ha-tov*. Therefore, God created both evil and good inclinations in humans from the very beginning.

Other rabbis, however, claimed that the *yetzer ha-rah* and *yetzer ha-tov* become active in people only upon reaching the age of maturity. In the Jewish tradition, boys reach their legal and social majority, on their thirteenth birthdays, when they reach Bar Mitzvah age. On the contrary, girls reach Bat Mitzvah age at twelve years old, corresponding to their earlier physical maturation. Becoming Bar or Bat Mitzvah literally means to become a "son [or daughter] of the commandments." This is the age when the obligation to observe the Jewish tradition devolves to young people. Given that the beginning of the teen years is also frequently the time when young people begin to assert their independence in sometimes rebellious ways, perhaps there is some truth to the following rabbinic passage:

> "Better a poor but wise child than an old but foolish king" (Ecclesiastes 4:13) [What is the "poor and wise child" referred to in this verse?] This is the good inclination. Why is it called a "child"? Because it only attaches itself to people from the age of 13 years and onward. And why is it called "poor"? Because not everyone listens to it! And why is it called "wise"? Because it teaches people the right way [to live].
>
> "An old and foolish king"—this is the evil inclination. Why is it called "king"? Because all obey it. Why is it

> called "old"? Because it attaches itself to people from youth to old age. Why is it called "foolish"? Because it teaches people the way of evil. [Ecclesiastes Rabba 4:13, 1]

Based on a verse from the book of Ecclesiastes, a compilation of wise and insightful sayings attributed to King Solomon at various stages of his life, the Rabbis claimed that this verse—it is far better to be a wise child than a foolish king—was an allegorical statement referring to the good and evil inclinations. The Rabbis then decoded each word in the verse and explained how it refers to either the good or evil inclination, noting especially that *yetzer ha-rah* only asserts its force over people from the age of 13 onward. The beginning of puberty is often characterized as the period when sexual hormones begin to affect the social and physical behavior of young people. Therefore, it is not so surprising that the Rabbis asserted that sexuality was a function of the *yetzer ha-rah*.

The relationship between sexuality and the *yetzer ha-rah* is complex. Afterall, how can an urge which leads to the procreation and perpetuation of the human race be considered evil? The Rabbis pondered this same question and arrived at surprising results:

> [Once, the Jewish people] said, "Let the evil inclination be handed over to us." They prayed and he was given to them. But the prophet [Elijah] warned them:

> "Understand that if you kill the evil inclination, the whole world will collapse."
>
> Nevertheless, they imprisoned the evil inclination for three days. But when they looked for a fresh egg, none could be found in all the land of Israel. "What shall we do?" the people asked each other. "Shall we kill him? But without the evil inclination, the world cannot survive." They said, "Shall we pray for partial leniency [allow him to live but pray that he not be allowed to tempt people]? God would not permit such a thing!" [Therefore, they decided] to put out his eyes and let him go. (Tractate *Yoma* 69a-b)

In this unusual story, the Jewish people temporarily had the power to receive whatever they prayed for—in this case, dominion over the the *yetzer ha-rah*, which was personified as an actual entity. However, they were cautioned that their actions could have disastrous consequences because of the importance of *yetzer ha-rah* as a life force. And in fact, after imprisoning the *yetzer ha-rah* for three days, the results of this incarceration are dramatically demonstrated by a lack of fresh eggs. The Rabbis erroneously assumed that without sexual relations chickens would not lay eggs. Despite the fact that this is not true, the point of the story is easily understood. By preventing the *yetzer ha-rah* from functioning, the vital life force active in the world of both humans and animals was removed resulting in a temporary cessation of all procreation. In a mythic ending, the Jewish people merely blinded the *yetzer ha-rah* and let it go. In other words, they ensured that the *yetzer ha-rah* would affect all people and creatures equally. Being unable to see, the *yetzer ha-rah* would not differentiate between young and old, men and women, wise or foolish. All humans would be subject to its hold.

Although there are dangers and difficulties in being human, one of them being subject to the sway of the *yetzer ha-rah*, it is necessary for the survival of humanity and all life. For even righteous, praise-worthy actions contain some aspect of the *yetzer ha-rah* as a goal or motivation. In fact, the Rabbis even understood the evil inclination to be essentially good! "Rabbi Nachman the son of Shmuel . . . said: "[And God saw all that He had made, and] found it very good." (Genesis 1:31) This refers to the good inclination. "*And* found it very good."—This is the evil inclination!" (Genesis Rabba 9:7) As we have seen previously, the Rabbis saw every letter in the Torah as significant and worthy of interpretation. In this case, Rabbi Nachman noted that after having created humanity, God commented on God's own handiwork by declaring it "very good." This phrase, by itself, was understood by Rabbi Nachman to refer to God's having created the good inclination in human beings. "Very good" then referred to the goodness of the good inclination. However, this is not the complete phrase. The full verse reads, "And God saw all that He had made, *and* found it very good." In Hebrew, the word "and" is indicated by the addition of a single letter. Rabbi Nachman interpreted this single letter, meaning, "and," to refer to God's creation of the evil inclination in addition to the good inclination. In which case, Rabbi Nachman put the radical assessment of the goodness of the evil inclination into own God's mouth! However, Rabbi Nachman's creative exposition did not go unchallenged. The passage continues:

> [An objection was raised] "Can it really be that the evil inclination was considered [by God] to be 'very good'?! This is astonishing!"
>
> [Rabbi Nachman answered,] "Were it not for the evil inclination, no man would build a house, marry a wife, or beget children or engage in commerce. And this is just what King Solomon said, 'I have seen that all labor and skillful enterprise comes from men's envy of each other.'" [Ecclesiastes 4:4]

Rabbi Nachman defended his position and justified it with an additional proof. Without the *yetzer ha-rah*, which as we saw above is a vital life force active throughout the human and animal world, there would be no productive activities in human society. The final quote from Ecclesiastes, attributed to King Solomon, puts a particularly interesting spin on Rabbi Nachman's position. Perhaps Rabbi Nachman is saying that were it not for envy, material desires, greed, or lust, no man would ever establish a home, marry and raise children, or engage in business. Far from being evil, the *yetzer ha-rah* is a necessary and crucial component of human life—both in the social and economic realms as well as the sexual.

However, no matter how natural and uniquely human it may be to harbor sexual desires, pursuing a life of romance is not without its risks. When we open ourselves up to the possibility of love, then we must be prepared to expose our vulnerabilities in order to build a relationship based on true intimacy.

13

Holiness and Sexuality

The great paradox about sexuality is that as we expose ourselves to progressively closer levels of intimacy in the creation of a relationship, there is greater potential for negative exploitation. Sexual relationships are not all equal in the Jewish tradition. Ideally, the greater the degree of intimacy, the greater the degree of holiness.

In fact, it is possible to create a stepladder of holiness based on various kinds of sexual relationships as follows:

Marriage

Engagement

Exclusive, long-term relationships

Serial, monogamous relationships

Casual sexual encounters

Adultery

Incest

Rape

This series of steps represents one possible interpretation of sexuality in the Jewish tradition and its relationship to holiness. While it is possible to insert a great deal more steps in this staircase, these levels portray a rather wide and representative spectrum of sexual liaisons between people.

Marital sex is at the top of this Jewish ladder of holiness and sexuality because the Hebrew word for marriage is *kiddushin*, which means "holiness." The Torah commands the Jewish people to strive for holiness in numerous places. God tells the Israelites, "You shall sanctify yourselves and by holy, for I am holy." (Leviticus 11:44) Biblical scholars have long noted that one of the literal meanings of the Hebrew word for holy, *kadosh*, is to be set apart—that is, to be special or elevated. This meaning of *kadosh* is evident in other places where the term is applied:

- The day of *Shabbat* is called *kadosh* when God declares, "Remember the Sabbath day and keep it holy (*kadosh*)." (Exodus 20:8) This means that the *Shabbat* is to be set apart from all the other days of the week. In fact, the sanctification of the wine made on *Shabbat* is called *kiddush*, which also means holiness or separateness. Therefore, in this situation, *kadosh* refers to separate, or holy time.
- The Temple in Jerusalem was called the *Beit ha-Mikdash*, (Mishnah *Sukkah* 3:12 and other places),

which means "the house of holiness." Therefore, the Temple, as God's symbolic dwelling place on earth, was the house which was to be set apart from other places. In this situation, *kadosh* refers to separate or holy space.

- In the face of death, Jews celebrate the holiness of life by reciting the *Kaddish* in honor of those who have passed away. The *Kaddish*, however, never mentions death. Rather, the prayer is entirely about God and God's holiness. Therefore, the *kaddish* sanctifies God who is eternal, and therefore separate and distinct from human beings who are mortal.

Therefore, the more exclusive a sexual relationship is, the holier it is in the Jewish tradition. Marriage is the highest step in this staircase because it is an exclusive relationship between two people who publicly and legally commit themselves to, hopefully, a loving and permanent relationship. The next step below marriage is engagement, because this is the prelude to marriage, when a couple has not yet legally committed to an exclusive relationship but both have publicly declared their intentions to do so. The next step below engagement is exclusive, long-term relationships. While a couple may indeed be committed to each other and the relationship may indeed be exclusive, neither party has any formal, public, or legal guarantee that this may always be the case. Therefore, while it still may be loving relationship, it must be considered less holy than those above.

Serial, monogamous relationships may be based on deep friendship and even love, but they cannot be considered particularly holy relationships. The level of intimacy may vary from couple to couple, but such relationships are by definition short-term, and lacking commitment. While the previous relationships mentioned above on the staircase of holiness and sexuality may begin initially as a short-term, monogamous relationship, until such a relationship deepens and becomes more serious involving greater commitment, intimacy, and vulnerability, it must still be considered less holy than those above it.

The next step below would be a casual sexual relationship: a short-term, perhaps even anonymous, sexual encounter. In this case, it is doubtful how well the partners even know each other. Therefore, the only basis for their relationship may be simply physical attraction. Because the partners have no chance to know one another, no basis for love to grow, and therefore no revelation of vulnerability to permit greater intimacy, such a relationship is far from holy.

The bottom three steps in this staircase are perhaps the antithesis of romantic, sexual relationships. Adultery, while it may contain elements of great intimacy and vulnerability, is not only immoral, but is frequently based on deception, and violates the most important component of a holy relationship, exclusive commitment. Incest and rape are not only illegal, but are examples of non-consensual sex where sex is wielded as a means of control. Therefore, they are the lowest and basest forms of sexual contact.

A holy relationship in the Jewish tradition is one where the partners are intimate with one another and share their vulnerabilities in a safe and supportive environment. Intimacy does not have to refer to sexual behavior. In fact, in order to achieve a truly holy relationship, intimacy should first be established through sharing emotional experiences and secrets in a trusting, supportive environment. Marriage counselors and therapists often note that successful relationships should begin first with emotional intimacy, which is then ultimately expressed through greater physical intimacy. The paradoxical aspect of this process is that the greater the level of intimacy—both emotional and physical—the more vulnerable we become to our partners. Exposing one's vulnerabilities is risky business. Ideally, the exposure of vulnerability should lead to the creation of a deep and profound foundation of trust and mutual confidence, from which to build an exclusive, loving, committed, and holy relationship. However, this is not often the case.

Sadly, many people tend to suffer from guilt, shame, embarrassment, and depression when first exploring sexuality. The less intimate and committed the relationship, the greater the chance for pain and humiliation. While both animals and humans can have sex, only humans have the potential to raise the sexual act above the biological level by imbuing it with spiritual significance and holiness. However, sex performed outside of the context of a committed relationship detracts from the holiness of sexuality and instead, brings it down to the level of mere promiscuity, called *z'nut* in Hebrew. The word *z'nut* is derived from another Hebrew word, *zonah* which means prostitute. Therefore, *z'nut* is degraded sex that serves no purpose other than immediate physical gratification.

In fact, the Torah explicitly forbids prostitution. "Do not degrade your daughter and make her a harlot, lest the land fall into harlotry and the land be filled with depravity." (Leviticus 19:29) It is interesting to note that the Torah presents this prohibition from the perspective of a father seeing his daughter as a potential prostitute, which might increase the revulsion a man could have when contemplating a visit to a prostitute. However, this prohibition against prostituting one's children did not prevent people from visiting prostitutes. One fascinating story in the Talmud describes such a situation and highlights the emotional vulnerability that one is subjected to when engaging in sex for purely physical satisfaction.

> It was said of Rabbi Eleazer ben Dordia that there was not a single prostitute in the entire world that he had not visited. Once, on hearing that there was a

> certain prostitute in one of the towns by the sea who would only accept a purse full of coins for her hire, he took a purse full of coins and crossed seven rivers for her sake. As he was with her, she emitted wind [vaginal flatulence]. She said, "Just as this [wind] which blew forth will never return to its [original] place, so too will Eleazar ben Dordia never be received in repentance [by God]." [Tractate *Avodah Zarah* 17a]

The prostitute was apparently so embarassed and humiliated by this situation that she cursed Rabbi Eleazer ben Dordia. Using her experience as the vehicle for her comparison, she condemned Rabbi Eleazer to a life, and perhaps even an afterlife, in which he would be denied God's acceptance and forgiveness. Rabbi Eleazer also became a victim in this superficial sexual union for he took the prostitute's curse seriously and wandered in despair, trying to seek divine repentance for a life filled with sexual debauchery. The passage continues:

> He then went and sat between two hills and mountains and exclaimed, "Hills and mountains! Plead for [divine] mercy for me [from God]!" They answered him, "How can we plead [for divine mercy] for you when we are in need of it ourselves! As it says, 'For the mountains shall melt and the hills will crumble [at the end of days]. . . .'" [Isaiah 54:10]

Pleading for the mountains and hills to intercede on his behalf, Rabbi Eleazer's plea was rejected. Quoting a verse from Isaiah in which the prophet proclaims that in a future time, even the mountains and hills will be reduced to level ground, the mountains and hills explain that they are just as much in need of divine intercession on their own behalf as Rabbi Eleazar.

So he turned to help elsewhere, unfortunately, with similar results:

> So he said, "Heaven and earth! Plead for [divine] mercy for me [from God]!" They answered, "How can we plead [for divine mercy] for you when we are in need of it ourselves! As it says, 'For the heavens shall vanish away like smoke and the earth will wear away like an old garment [at the end of days]. . . .'" [Isaiah 51:6]
>
> So he said, "Sun and moon! Plead for [divine] mercy for me [from God]!" They answered, "How can we plead [for divine mercy] for you when we are in need of it ourselves! As it says, 'Then the moon shall be undone and the sun will be ashamed [at the end of days]. . . .'" (Isaiah 24:23)
>
> So he said, "Stars and planets! Plead for [divine] mercy for me [from God]!" They answered, "How can we plead [for divine mercy] for you when we are in need of it ourselves! As it says, 'And all of the hosts

> of heaven shall molder away [at the end of days]. . . .'" (Isaiah 34:4)
>
> So he said, "The matter then depends upon me alone." He lowered his head between his knees and groaned and cried until his soul departed. Then a divine voice issued from heaven and said, "Rabbi Eleazar ben Dordia has been invited into the World to Come!" (Tractate *Avodah Zarah* 17a)

Rabbi Eleazar ben Dordia was afraid that his prodigious promiscuity would preclude his ability to ultimately repent for his sins and be admitted into the spiritual world of reward, known in the rabbinic tradition as the World to Come. Only when Rabbi Eleazer recognized that he was solely responsible for his fate was he successful in achieving repentance, albeit at the cost of his life. Despite Rabbi Eleazer's past sexual transgressions, this story is instructive in that it indicates that people can learn from their mistakes and achieve full repentance while reinforcing the risks one takes on when eschewing exclusive relationships.

Biblical scholars surmise that in addition to finding prostitution morally abhorrent, the Torah forbid prostitution because it was associated with ancient Canaanite fertility practices. The Torah indicates this when it states, "No Israelite women shall be a cult prostitute, nor shall any Israelite man be a cult prostitute. You shall not bring the fee of a whore or the pay of a dog into the house of the Lord your God in fulfillment of any vow, for both are abhorrent to the Lord your God." (Deuteronomy 23:18–19) It is ironic that the terms used for both the male and female cultic prostitute in this passage are the Hebrew words *kadesh* and *kadesha*, derived from the word "holy." However, in this case, the term probably comes from the fact that ritual prostitutes were hired for sexual fertility rites in Canaanite temples. Not only did the Torah forbid Israelites from entering this profession, but even the earnings of such a cultic prostitute were proscribed from being used in any Israelite religious practice. The unusual phrase, "pay of a dog" is unclear, but some biblical scholars believe that this is simply a derogatory way to refer to a male cultic prostitute.

Whatever the circumstances might have been, prostitution was considered an unholy sexual liaison. Sex should be part of a committed, loving, and intimate relationship. However, negative sexual experiences can emotionally scar people for the rest of their lives. The Jewish tradition is particularly emphatic in its condemnation of immoral and hurtful sexual relations.

14

Sex that Hurts or Destroys

Immoral, illegal, and destructive sex is called *gilui arayot* in the Jewish tradition. This literally means the "exposing of nakedness." When anyone is exposed, they are made vulnerable. Therefore, *gilui arayot* refers to all forms of inappropriate sexual liaisons, such as rape, incest, and adultery. These are sexual liaisons which destroy bonds of trust and intimacy and take advantage of the victim's vulnerability, often leaving deep and long-lasting emotional scars and trauma.

The clearest example of why *gilui arayot* is prohibited occurs in the Torah where Joseph, serving as the head slave of the Egyptian Potiphar's house, refuses Potiphar's wife's sexual advances.

> He said to his master's wife, "Look, with me here, my master gives no thought to anything in this house, and all that he owns he has placed in my hands. He wields no more authority in this house than I, and he

> has withheld nothing from me except yourself, since you are his wife. How then could I do this most wicked thing, and sin before God?" [Genesis 39:8–9]

Joseph's refusal to engage in adultery is predicated on clear moral terms. First, he indicates to that he would be betraying his master's trust by sleeping with his wife. Second, because she is Potiphar's wife, Joseph has no right to have sex with her. Finally, Joseph states that such an act would be wicked, a "sin before God." All of these components are the essence of *gilui arayot* in the Torah.

The most terrible form of *gilui arayot* is rape. However, the Torah is not as ethically clear as we might hope in this situation. Rape only seems to apply if a woman is engaged. The Torah states,

> But if the man comes upon the engaged girl in the open country, and the man lies with her by force, only the man who lay with her shall die, but you shall do nothing to the girl. The girl did not incur the death penalty, for this case is like that of a man attacking another and murdering him. He came upon her in the open; though the engaged girl cried for help, there was no one to save her. [Deuteronomy 22:25–27]

In this case, a woman who is already betrothed to another is raped by a man beyond city limits. Because her potential cries for help could not have been heard, she is considered blameless in this situation and her attacker suffers capital punishment. However, this situation only applies if the woman was already engaged. If she is a virgin—that is, an available, unengaged woman—and she is raped, whether in a town or in the country, the outcome is very different: "If a man came upon a virgin who is not engaged and he seized her and lay with her, and they are discovered, the man who lay with her shall pay the girl's father fifty shekels of silver, and she shall be his wife. Because he has violated her, he can never have the right to divorce her." (Deuteronomy 22:28–29) Rape of an available woman is thus considered an illegal seizure, whereby a man attempts to acquire a wife against her parents' will or her own. The implication is that sexual relations with an available woman—whether consensual or not—constitute a semi-legitimate avenue to marriage. The fact that the man is not condemned to death as the attacker was in the previous passage indicates that the Torah does not consider this a case of rape. Rather, the man is fined fifty silver shekels—which is paid to the woman's father—for pursuing a socially and economically inappropriate path to consummating a marriage. The father is considered the victim here, because the man did not follow the social and economic traditions of that time: namely, bargaining on a bride price. Because the daughter is no longer a virgin, the bride price that she could fetch would be severely reduced and any potential suitors would probably lose interest in her. Therefore, the Torah probably felt that it was in the woman's best financial interests to be married to this man in order to secure a husband at all. And the additional penalty that the man had to accept was the inability to divorce this woman due to the inappropriate way he made her his wife. The wishes or feelings of the woman are not mentioned in the Torah. Whatever we as modern Jews may feel about this situation, the Torah assumed that it was looking after the woman's best interests in this case, securing her life-long security with a man who had no choice but to support her the rest of his life.

Although rape is now understood to be a crime of violence where sex is used as a weapon for control, this understanding was unknown in biblical times. However, the Rabbis of the Talmud did recognize the seriousness of rape and even compared it to a crime as heinous as murder. In fact, the Rabbis ruled in the Talmud that rape is tantamount to murder. Therefore, one can kill a pursuing rapist just as one is permitted to kill a pursuing murderer, a *rodef*: "These [people] can be saved [from committing a transgression] even at the cost of their life: one who pursues his fellow person to kill him, one who pursues a man [for homosexual rape], or who pursues a betrothed maiden [to rape her]." (Tractate *Sanhedrin* 73a) It is unusual that the Talmud presents this list of people who can be stopped through deadly force; in other words, it is acceptable to kill people in the act of committing these crimes, in order to "save" them from the sin of the crime. However, the Talmud understands such preemptive killing as a way to safeguard the criminal's spiritual integrity before he actually commits the horrible crime. In this passage, bystanders and witnesses are permitted to use all force at their disposal to prevent murder, homosexual rape, or rape of a betrothed woman. It should be noted that the woman *must be* betrothed, or even already married, because as noted above, rape only applies to a woman who is no longer available to another man. If the woman is available, then it is not considered rape. Despite this glaring omission, the Rabbis did treat rape seriously and equated it with murder.

In fact, the Rabbis were so repelled by the crime of rape that they ruled that even if a woman consented to her own rape—if such a thing is possible—she was not held culpable for her actions. In other words, the Rabbis treated every situation of rape as involuntary, non-consensual sex. (This, sadly, contrasts with many rape trials in recent times where any indication of a woman's non-resistance is held up as evidence of her consent and used to exonerate her attacker.) Despite the vehemence of the Rabbi's insistence upon the rape victim's innocence, one solitary talmudic rabbi held that a woman should be held responsible for her own rape! However, as we shall soon see, his opinion was roundly attacked and dismissed. The Talmud states:

"The father of Shmuel taught, 'A woman who is raped is forbidden to her husband, for perhaps the beginning was by force but in the end she went along willingly.'" (Tractate *Ketubot* 51a)

Although we may view this as terribly unfair, the Rabbis ruled that when a married woman had an affair she was considered ritually defiled as result of the interruption in her marital sexual fidelity. Therefore she was not permitted to return to her husband and resume her previous sexual relationship. Although their marriage continued, their sexual relationship was no longer sanctioned. This Rabbi above, however, tried to extend this prohibition even to women who had been raped. This did not go without challenge:

> "This disagrees with Rava, for Rava ruled, 'In all cases where the beginning is by force and in the end she goes along willingly, even if she says [to her rescuers] "leave him alone, for if this had not happened I would have hired him!" She is [still] permitted to her husband.' [The Rabbis then asked] 'What is the reason for this? Her sexual drive overpowered her.'" (Tractate *Ketubot* 51a)

The talmudic sage Rava decreed that no situation of rape could ever be considered consensual. Rava illustrated his view with a bizarre and offensive hypothetical situation in which a woman hires someone to rape her! According to the passage, even if this woman were interrupted in the act of being raped and then explained to her would-be rescuers that the act of rape had become somehow become consensual sex in the course of the rape, this would *still* not cause her to be ritually defiled and she would be able to return to her husband. That is to say, even when a woman explicitly claims that a rape was consensual, the Rabbis refuse to accept this! The other, later Rabbis, attempting to deduce the reasoning behind Rava's decree, explained that a woman who may in fact end up consenting to her own rape cannot be considered as having made a rationally balanced decision. This is because according to these Rabbis, her decision was deemed as if compelled by her internal sexual desire.

In the Jewish tradition, when people make decisions under duress, they are not considered culpable for their judgment. Once again, this interpretation is based on the belief that a woman can become sexually aroused during her own rape, deciding to give into her attacker. The interpretation also implies that a woman's sexual desires can overcome her intellectual ability to make rational choices for herself. Yet, despite the strange, and even misogynistic, framework of this reasoning, it articulates important protective principles for women in the Jewish tradition: namely, rape is never consensual, and a woman can never be held culpable for her own victimhood even if she herself tried to waive it.

Long before Western society recognized a wife's right to refuse sexual advances of her husband, the Rabbis of the Talmud went further in support of rape victims, determining that even a husband is forbidden to force his wife to have sexual relations against her will. "Rami bar Hama, citing Rabbi Assi, ruled, 'A man is forbidden to force his wife to fulfill the marital commandment [sex].' Rabbi Yehoshua ben Levi taught, 'Anyone who forces his wife to fulfill the marital commandment will produce children who are not "fit."'" (Tractate *Eruvin* 100b) Although the Rabbis did not establish marital rape as a crime punishable by the courts, Rabbi Yehoshua ben Levi at least tried to add a morally compelling threat to his prohibition by warning husbands that any children conceived through marital rape will be deformed or blemished in some way, either physically or morally. It is unclear whether this prohibition was effective, but it certainly indicates that the Rabbis tried to work within the moral sphere to prevent marital rape.

An equally horrifying sexual crime is incest; violating familial bonds is the ultimate act of exploiting another person's vulnerability. Leviticus (Chapter 18) specifies in great detail each and every incestuous relationship forbidden by the Torah. Intercourse with all members of one's nuclear family is prohibited, as well as intercourse with their spouses. In addition, sexual relations with stepchildren, aunts, uncles, and inlaws are also not permitted. Because the Torah already assumes the prohibition against adultery and incest, these particular laws are assumed to be referring to the interdiction against potential marriage partners. Speculating about the underlying causes for prohibiting incest, Rambam wrote:

> The female relatives whom a man may not marry are alike in this respect—as a rule they are constantly together with him in his house; they would easily listen to him, and do what he desires; they are near at hand, and he would have no difficulty in procuring them. No judge could blame him if [merely] found in their company. If to these relatives the same law applied as to all other unmarried women, if we were allowed to marry any of them, and were only precluded from sexual intercourse with them without marriage, most people would constantly become guilty of misconduct with them. [*Guide to the Perplexed* 3:49]

In other words, the potential for exploitation when two members of the same family live in the same household is sufficient reason for prohibiting incest. No matter what the blood ties might be, Rambam stated that such a relationship takes unfair advantage of another person's vulnerabilities by abusing ties of blood and familial friendship.

Adultery, one more illicit sex crime that preys on another's vulnerability, is the only sexual transgression mentioned in the Ten Commandments. (Exodus 20:13 and Deuteronomy 5:17) Not only is adultery forbidden, but secretly coveting another's wife is considered an equally severe transgression. (Exodus 20:14) Hence, adultery is the ultimate crime against a partner and a family because it directly threatens the stability of individual families as well as of society as a whole.

Adultery, however, has a very specific definition in the Jewish tradition. According to the Torah, a man is permitted to have more than one wife. The Torah even stipulates that when a man takes another wife, he cannot withhold clothing, or sexual relations from his first wife. (Exodus 21:10) However, a woman can have only one husband, as implied in the case of a woman whom her husband suspects has committed adultery with another man (Numbers 5:11 ff); in this passage adultery applies only to a woman who is married to another man. As the Torah states: "If a man commits adultery with a married woman—another's wife—the adulterer and the adulteress shall be put to death." (Leviticus 20:10) The Torah does not seem to care if the adulterer is already married or not, for polygamy was permitted. However, a woman cannot have more than one husband. Thus, one of the problems many modern Jews have with the biblical and rabbinic concept of adultery is its sexism. Adultery only applies to a married woman, since it was theoretically possible for a man to have more than one wife. It was not until the decree of Rabbenu Gershom around 1000 C.E. that polygamy was abolished in the Jewish tradition.

The children of an adulterous sexual union—that is, when a married woman has children with a man other than her husband—are called *mamzerim*, literally, "bastards." However, a *mamzer* is not merely an illegitimate child in the Jewish tradition, but he carries a life-long legacy of discrimination. A *mamzer* is a full Jew in every way except one—a *mamzer* cannot marry another Jew. The Torah states, "No *mamzer* shall be admitted into the congregation of the Lord. None of his descendants, even in the tenth generation, shall be admitted into the congregation of the Lord." (Deuteronomy 23:3) If a *mamzer* were to marry another legitimately born Jew and have children, their children would also be *mamzerim*. In fact, a *mamzer* can only marry another *mamzer*, however, their children would also be *mamzerim*, based on the talmudic principle—"In every case where there is a valid betrothal and one [or both of the partners] are themselves the product of a sin [that is, are *mamzerim*], the offspring follow after the disqualified parent." (Mishnah *Kiddushin* 3:12)

Perhaps the reason for such harsh and punitive laws regarding *mamzerim* was to deter and thoroughly discourage adultery. The Torah and the Rabbis hoped that the dire consequences which they would bequeath to their offspring would deter adulterers from committing sexual crimes. Because these regulations punish children for the crimes of parents, some might argue that they are contrary to the spirit of the law in the Torah that states, "Parents shall not be put to death for children, nor children be put to death for parents: a person shall be put to death only for his own crime." (Deuteronomy 24:16) Although not a death penalty, the laws discriminating against a *mamzer* are indeed harsh and punitive primarily to the children.

The issue of *mamzerim* is one which still troubles modern Jewry today. Perhaps the lesson we should draw from these texts is that if a marital relationship degenerates to such a point a that one or both of the partners are considering adultery, and no reconciliation is possible, divorce should be considered. While every attempt should always be made to preserve a marriage, committing adultery is a significant sign that something has gone wrong in the marital relationship and needs to be resolved.

The ideal sexual relationship in the Jewish tradition is marriage. However, before people make the commitment to marry, they often explore sexuality in less committed relationships. Surprisingly enough, the Jewish tradition has much to say about nonmarital sexuality.

15

Nonmarital Sex

Although the ideal of the Jewish tradition is that sexual activity should be reserved exclusively for one's spouse, obviously not everyone can, or will, abstain from sex until marriage. Given the reality of our society, even though parents and authority figures may stress and encourage abstinence, the reality is that many teenagers and young adults will experiment and engage in sexual activity long before they marry. Given the Jewish tradition's ideal of sexual relations only within a marital context, it may seem strange to discover that there are quite a number of Jewish texts which deal with nonmarital, especially premarital, sexuality.

Nonmarital relationships are treated matter-of-factly in the Bible. For example, Judah, the son of Jacob, has intercourse with his daughter-in-law, Tamar, because he thinks she is a harlot. (Genesis 38:15 ff) King David shares his bed in his old age with the young Abishag the Shunamite in order to stay warm. (I Kings 1:1–4) In each case, the sexual liaison is treated lightly, even casually.

The Torah's main concern regarding nonmarital sexuality was that a young woman would lose her virginity, which in biblical society constituted her value as a candidate for marriage. A woman's virginity was even taken into account in the *ketubah*, the wedding contract. According to the Mishnah, a virgin was to receive two hundred silver coins if divorced or widowed, while a non-virgin or divorcé only received only one hundred silver coins. (Mishnah *Ketubot* 1:2) Thus, nonmarital sex was not only seen in moral terms, but also in a financial and social context. In fact, it is possible to claim that the Torah never explicitly forbids premarital sex, for every such instance was viewed as an act of establishing a marital bond. As we saw previously, the Torah states, "If a man comes upon a virgin who is not engaged and he seizes her and lies with her, and they are discovered, the man who lay with her shall pay the girl's father fifty shekels of silver, and she shall be his wife. Because he has violated her, he can never have the right to divorce her." (Deuteronomy 22:28–29)

Although this is presented in the context of rape, it is clear that the very act of having sex establishes the marital bond. The Talmud states that among the various legitimate ways that a man may establish a marital relationship with a woman is to have sex with her. The

Mishnah states, "A woman is acquired in three ways: by a document, silver, or sexual relations." (Mishnah *Kiddushin* 1:1) Because women were not recognized as legally or financially independent in ancient times, marriage was viewed as a form of acquisition for the man. The document refers to the *ketubah*, marital contract and the silver refers to some gift or item of value that a man might give to a woman as a token of marriage. This method of marriage is still preserved in the customary exchange of wedding rings. Finally, having sex with a woman was another means by which a man could marry the woman. (Cohabitation without the benefit of sanctioned nuptials is still recognized in many states today as common law marriage.) Thus, in biblical times there was no such thing as premarital sex for the very act of having sex transformed it into a marital bond.

However, long after the time of the Bible, the Rabbis of the Talmud explicitly prohibited premarital and nonmarital sexual relations. In one amusing story, the Rabbis refused to countenance a nonmarital sexual relationship, even when it endangered the life of one young man:

> There was once a case where a man cast his eyes upon a woman who aroused a fire in his heart. When the doctors were sent for, they said, "His only cure is that she have sex with him." The sages said, "Let him

> die and not have sex!" [The doctors] said, "Then let her stand before him naked." [The sages replied], "Let him die and not have her stand naked before him!" [The doctors said] "Let her (at least) speak with him from behind a fence. [The sages replied] "Let him die and not have her speak with him from behind a fence!" [Tractate *Sanhedrin* 75a]

It would appear that this situation involved an unmarried man and a single, available woman. In this case, the Rabbis were prepared to let the man die rather than allow him to engage in nonmarital sexual relations. However, because this situation was so unclear, later rabbis argued about the specific circumstances of the case. They wondered if the Rabbis forbid such a sexual union because the woman might actually have been married. The passage continues:

> Now Rabbi Yaakov and Rabbi Shmuel bar Nachmani argued about this case. One said that this woman was married, but the other claimed that she was unmarried. It makes sense [that the sages prohibited sexual relations] if she was married, but if she was unmarried, why such severity? Rabbi Pappa said, "Because of the disgrace to her family." Rabbi Aha son of Rabbi Ika said, "[The sages forbid such a union so] that the daughters of Israel should not be promiscuous in their sexuality." (Tractate *Sanhedrin* 75a)

It is clear that the Rabbis refused to permit this sexual union in order to protect the family name of the woman, and to prevent the moral dissolution of Jewish women in general. Here, the Rabbis went far beyond the biblical lassitude regarding nonmarital sexuality. In order to prevent premarital sex, the Rabbis advocated early marriage for both boys and girls in order to confine their sexuality entirely to the domain of marriage. The Rabbis claimed that "at eighteen years of age, [a man is ready for] marriage." (Mishnah *Pirkei Avot* 4:23)

However, it appears that the Rabbis had little patience for those men who did not marry shortly thereafter. They seemed to run out of patience after only two years. "[Rav Huna] taught, 'Whoever is twenty years of age and is not married spends all his days in sin.' [An anonymous rabbi then asked] 'In sin? Can you really think so?! Rather, say instead, he spends all his days in *thoughts* of sin!'" (Tractate *Kiddushin* 29b) Rav Huna's original statement implies that if a man has not married after turning eighteen and before turning twenty, he spends his time either masturbating or visiting prostitutes. The vulgarity of this suggestion was immediately challenged and emended so that rather than implying young men would actually engage in sinful actions, they instead would probably spend their days in sexual fantasies.

Another rabbi took up this same theme of impatience in waiting for young men to marry. The passage continues: "Rava said, 'Until the age of twenty, the Holy One, blessed be He, sits and waits, [thinking,] "When will he take a wife?" As soon as one attains twenty and has not married, God exclaims, "Blasted be his bones!"'"

Despite this pressure upon young men to marry early, the Rabbis established a highly moral, legal presumption that a Jewish man would never have sexual relations with a single woman unless it were expressly for the purposes of marriage. Whether this was true or not, it was their official position, perhaps to attempt to avoid the issue of nonmarital promiscuity. The Mishnah explains, "If a man has divorced his wife but then stays with her overnight in an inn, the House of Shammai says that she does not require a second *get* from him. The House of Hillel says that she does require a second *get* from him." (Mishnah *Gittin* 8:9) The House of Shammai assumed that a man who had the opportunity to have sexual relations with his ex-wife would never take advantage of their previous relationship and do so. Because the act of sex constitutes a valid and binding means by which to effect marriage, the ex-husband would not have to give his ex-wife a *get*, the official document of divorce, since they did not have sexual relations. However, the House of Hillel assumed that an ex-husband would indeed have sex with his ex-wife if he were able to and therefore, in the process, their previous marital status would be reconstituted as a result of their sexual union. Therefore, the man would have to give another document of divorce, a *get*, to his wife in order to once again divorce her. The Rabbis of the Talmud analyzed this passage and came to the following conclusions: "The House of Shammai holds that a man [in such a case] would not engage in promiscuous sexual intercourse, whereas the House of Hillel holds that a man would [in fact] engage in sexual intercourse [but only for the sake of re-betrothal]." (Tractate *Gittin* 81b)

Rambam, along with the talmudic Rabbis, also had no qualms about prohibiting nonmarital sex. However, he claimed that prior to the giving of the Torah, nonmarital sex was permitted. However, he only appeared to understand this in the framework of prostitution:

> Previous to the giving of the Torah, a man would meet a woman in the market and if he wanted her, he would give her money, and have sex with her, and then go on his way. And this [woman] was called a *kedesha* [a temple prostitute in pagan temples]. However, once the Torah was given, this was forbidden, as it says, "No Israelite woman shall be a cultic prostitute." (Deuteronomy 23:18) Therefore, anyone who has sex with a woman merely for promiscuous purposes without betrothal is to be lashed according to the Torah because he had sex with a *kedesha* [which is forbidden]. (Mishneh Torah, *Hilchot Ishut* 1:4)

Everyone did not agree with Rambam and his claim that the Torah prohibited promiscuous sex. Rabbi Abraham ben David, a medieval rabbi who was one of Rambam's sharpest critics, disagreed with the passage above, although he added in his own unusual interpretation of a man's ability to have non-marital sexual relations:

> This situation [described above] is impossible! There is no such thing as a *kedesha*! Rather, this is simply an accessible woman who happens to be available to any man. And if she secluded herself with a man [for the purposes of having sex], she receives neither lashes nor has she violated any Torah prohibition. She is, instead, a *pilegesh* [concubine], which is written about in the Bible. And linguistic scholars claim that the word *pilegesh* is a combined word and consists of the words, *pi* [which means "according to"] and *shegel* [which means "delight"] who is available at times for [sexual delight]. She takes care of a [man's] home and occasionally [occupies] his bed. (Mishneh Torah, *Hilchot Ishut* 1:4, RAVAD)

Neither Rambam nor Rabbi Abraham ben David could have anticipated the complexity of modern society and the sexual revolution which vastly liberalized the sexual mores of our times. However, they each recognized different kinds of nonmarital sex within the social and moral constructs of their time and within the Jewish tradition and each struggled to articulate an appropriate vision of sexual relations. Despite the Rabbis' strong aversion to non-marital sexuality, they could not help but confront the fact that the Torah never explicitly forbids such relationships.

Perhaps the Rabbis were threatened by nonmarital sex not because it is immoral or unethical, but because it undermines the ideal of Jewish holiness of marital sexuality. Perhaps the Rabbis worried that if sex was not limited to marriage, why would people bother to marry at all? If sexual fulfillment could be obtained outside of marriage, then the ideal of marital sexuality might be ignored or abandoned. Of course, it is obvious that the Torah never saw the need to prohibit premarital sex because biblical society could not even conceive of such relationships. Therefore, the Rabbis attempted to forbid premarital and nonmarital sex in order to safeguard the ideal of Jewish marriage, the highest step in the staircase of holiness and sexuality.

16

Marital Sex

The most common answer that people provide when asked the purpose of marriage in the Jewish tradition is naturally enough procreation. While they are not wrong, there are two other equally important goals of marriage in Judaism: namely, partnership and pleasure.

The first goal of marriage enunciated in the Torah is actually partnership. As God says about Adam, the first man, "It is not good for the man to be alone. I will make a fitting helper for him." (Genesis 2:18) In this story of the creation of human beings, Eve was created to provide companionship for Adam. The assumption was that God was creating a marraige partner, so that the first human beings could live out their lives in partnership, never being alone.

Another goal of marriage in Judaism is to provide mutual sexual pleasure for one's spouse. This is evident when the Torah lists those men who are exempt from being called to military service. The Torah states, "When a man has taken a bride, he shall not go out with the army or be assigned to it for any purpose; he shall be exempt one year for the sake of his household, to give happiness to the woman he has married." (Deuteronomy 24:5) This obligation, however, does not end with the first year of marriage, for it says in the Talmud, "Rava taught, 'Every man is obligated to rejoice his wife with the marital mitzvah [commandment].'" (Tractate *Pesachim* 72b) Since no time frame is given, this implies that a man is always required to engage in sexual relations with his wife in order to "give her happiness."

It is interesting to note that in the Jewish tradition, it is the man's obligation to engage in regular sexual relations with his wife, and to provide her sexual pleasure. This obligation is actually stipulated in the Torah, albeit in an unusual situation. In biblical times, a man could arrange to have a young Jewish woman serve in his household as an indentured handmaiden, for such women were considered eligible and legitimate partners in marriage. Perhaps it was even assumed that the master of the house took in the young woman intentionally for the purposes of marriage. However, if the master of the house did not want her for a wife, he could arrange to have his son marry her. The Torah states, "But if he designated her for his son, he shall deal with her as is the practice with free maidens. If he [the son] married another, he must not withhold from this one her food, her clothing, or her conjugal rights." (Exodus 21:9–10) The Rabbis understood this to mean that when a man takes a second wife he cannot in any way neglect his first wife. From here, the Rabbis established the three basic obligations for a husband to provide for his wife: food, clothing, and regular sexual relations. In fact, these basic rights of the wife are included in every traditional *ketubah*. The term used for regular sexual relations in the Torah, however, is somewhat unusual in Hebrew. The word *onah* literally means "her appointed time." Hence, the Rabbis actually determined the frequency that different couples should have marital sexual relations based on the occupation of the husband: "The times for marital relations spoken of in the Torah are: for [men of] independent means—once a day; for workmen—twice a week; for camel drivers—once every thirty days; for sailors—once every six months" [Mishnah *Ketubot* 5:6]

These regular times were not arbitrarily chosen. Men of independent means were required to have sex with their wives once a day since they did not work for a living and were home every night. Workmen, who were employed in the same city in which they lived, could return to their homes every night, but perhaps due to their hard physical labor, the Rabbis only required them to have sex with their wives twice a week. Camel drivers, who would often take long journeys across the desert in caravans on trade routes, could reasonably be expected to return home once a month, at which time they were required to have sex with their wives. The same applied for sailors who would journey off on longer voyages, but upon their return, they too were required to uphold their marital obligations.

Although the Torah and Talmud do not provide explicit instructions about how to go about engaging in marital sexual relations, The *Iggeret HaKodesh*, a Hebrew manuscript attributed to Moshe ben Nachman (Nachmanides), a Spanish rabbi in the thirteenth century, deals entirely with how to fulfill the commandment of marital sex. The *Iggeret HaKodesh* was studied by young men in late medieval times as preparation for their marriages. Valued as a holy "sex manual," this work laid out appropriate rules of not only sexual conduct but marital conduct in general. Nachmanides, writing to his brother on the occasion of the latter's marriage, advised him in all types of intimate matters. At one point he writes,

> A husband should speak to his wife with fitting words of erotic passion, and fear of the Lord. He must speak with her in the middle of the night. . . . A man should never force himself upon his wife and never overpower her, for the Holy Presence never rests upon one whose marital relations occur in the absence of desire, love, or free will. . . . He should never argue with his wife, and certainly never hit her on account of sexual matters. . . . Rather, you

> should act so that you will warm her heart by speaking to her flattering and seductive words. . . . A man should never have sexual relations with his wife while she is asleep, for then they cannot both agree to the act. It is far better . . . to arouse her with words that will soothe her and inspire passion in her. To conclude, when you are ready for sexual union, see that your wife's intentions combine with yours. Do not hurry to arouse her until she is receptive. Be calm, and as you enter the path of love and desire, let her "seeding" come first. . . . (*Iggeret HaKodesh*, Chapter 6)

Of particular interest is Nachmanides' exhortation for men to ensure that the pace of their lovemaking is equal to that of their wives, and the curious conclusion to the passage. Speaking euphemistically, Nachmanides was encouraging men to ensure that their wives achieved orgasm before themselves. This may not have simply been due to chivalry. The Rabbis believed that in order for healthy conception to occur, a woman must achieve orgasm first because she provided the raw materials for the embryo. The man's semen then provided the basic structure and outline of the baby's form.

Within the marital context, all forms of sexual pleasure are permitted. In fact, the Talmud explicitly declares that there are no required positions or acts of love that a husband or wife must engage in. It is completely up to the couple. This is clear from the following passage in the Talmud. However, the analogy is unusual and may be somewhat shocking: "Anything that a man wants to do with his wife—let him do. This can be compared to meat which comes from the butcher: If he wants to eat it with salt, let him eat! If he wants to eat it roasted, let him eat! If he wants to eat it cooked, let him eat! If he wants to eat it broiled, let him eat! And similarly with fish that comes from the fisherman." (Tractate *Nedarim* 20a–20b) It must be pointed out that the meat being spoken of here in this passage is not referring to the body of a woman. Although the Jewish tradition is male-centered, it is by no means misogynistic nor does it deny the humanity of any person. It would be offensive and antithetical to Jewish values not to see all people, men and women alike, as being created in the image of God.

On the contrary, the meat here refers to the sexual act itself. It is kosher meat, as the passage explicitly states, "meat which comes from the [kosher] butcher,"—that is, meat that has been slaughtered in the appropriate Jewish way so that it can be eaten and enjoyed by Jews. That is also why the passage refers to fish "that comes from the (kosher) fisherman." A kosher fish, one that has fins and scales (Leviticus 11:9) can be eaten, according to Rashi who comments on this talmudic passage, "in any way that they (Jews) want." (Tractate *Nedarim* 20b, Rashi) This is supported by Rabbenu Nissim, who also comments on this section of the Talmud, "fish that can be roasted or broiled as they like." (Tractate *Nedarim* 20b, Ran)

The kosher meat and kosher fish is analogous to "kosher" sex, that is, sexual relations between a husband and a wife. In dietary laws of keeping kosher, there is no one official way that kosher meat must be eaten. Once the animal has been slaughtered in the kosher manner and the meat prepared in the kosher way, Jews can cook and eat the meat any way that they so choose. The same is true of kosher fish after they have been caught. That is why the passage goes on at length to emphasize that the meat can be eaten salted, roasted, cooked, or broiled. This is a euphemism for the wide variety of sexual practices that a couple may indulge in as Rashi and Rabbenu Nissim imply.

Marital sex can be enjoyed in any position or manner that the couple wants. Like kosher meat, both of them are able to enjoy the "meal" together. Although directed at men, this sexual freedom applies to both husbands and wives together. Far from being anti-women, this passage is actually sexually liberating, enjoining a married couple to engage in whatever sexual positions or acts that they may so desire. In fact, the passage continues so as to emphasize this very freedom:

> "[Once] a woman came before Rebbi [Yehuda HaNasi] and said, 'Rebbi, I prepared a table for him and he overturned it.' He replied, 'My daughter, the

Torah permits you this! What do you want me to do?'"

In this passage, when the woman says that she prepared a table for her husband, it appears that she was prepared to have sexual intercourse in the missionary position. However, her husband, "overturned the table," meaning, he had sex with her in a different way. This reading is supported by Rabbenu Asher, a medieval talmudic commentator, who notes, "He had sexual relations with her not in the 'normal' way." (Tractate *Nedarim* 20b, Rosh) Modern talmudic scholarship also understands the ambiguous phrase, overturning the table" to refer to "anal intercourse, or . . . vaginal intercourse from behind, or even just . . . vaginal intercourse with the woman on top." (p. 110, *Carnal Israel: Reading Sex in Talmudic Culture*, Daniel Boyarin, University of California Press, Berkeley, 1993)

Later, the woman came to see Rebbi because she was not sure that what she and her husband did was permitted within the Jewish tradition. Therefore, Rebbi reassured the woman that such sexual activity is in fact permitted by the Torah and there is no need to involve him in these matters. Sexual relations are exclusively the province of the married couple. This passage implies that couples should not try to drag rabbis into their bedrooms!

Centuries later, Rambam clarified this liberal attitude towards sexual relations within a marital context when he wrote: "A man's wife is permitted to him. Therefore a man may do whatever he wishes with his wife. He may have intercourse with her at any time he wishes, and kiss her on whatever limb of her body he wants. He may have natural or unnatural sex, as long as he does not bring forth seed in vain." (Mishneh Torah, *Hilchot Issurei Biah* 21:10) Reverting back to male-centered language, Rambam clarifies that within marriage a couple can do whatever they want provided the man ultimately achieves orgasm while in the course of vaginal sex, ensuring the possibility of procreation. The Hebrew phrase which has been translated as "natural sex" literally means "in the way"—that is, the way of nature. "Unnatural sex," therefore is not in the way of nature. Rambam based himself here on a different section of the Talmud which discusses the biblical story of Er and Onan.

Er and Onan were the two older sons of Judah, the son of Jacob. For reasons which are not given in the Torah, Er was struck down by God before consummating his marriage with his wife, Tamar. At that time, the duty of marrying and raising children in the dead husband's name fell upon the next younger brother, Onan. The Torah explicitly states that "Onan, knowing that the seed would not count as his, let it spoil on the ground whenever he joined with his brother's wife, so as not to provide offspring for his brother." (Genesis 38:9) In other words, Onan practiced *coitus interrup-*

tus, or early withdrawal. For this sin, God struck down Onan as well.

The Rabbis assumed that both brothers were killed for having committed sexual crimes against God. In one brief passage, the Rabbis declared, "Er and Onan did not have sex in the [natural] way." (Tractate *Yevamot* 34b) Rabbi Shelomo Yitzchaki, the classic medieval commentator on the Torah and Talmud, known by the acronym Rashi, explained that unnatural sex here refers to "any place where insemination does not usually take place." (Rashi on Tractate *Yevamot* 34b) In other words, perhaps what Er and Onan practiced was not only early withdrawal, but also masturbation, oral sex, or anal sex. Therefore, unnatural sex, according to Rashi, is any sexual act where the man's orgasm occurs anywhere outside of the woman's vagina, thereby precluding conception.

Adding commentary to commentary, the *Tosafot*, the later medieval commentary on the Talmud, discussed the appropriateness of any married couple engaging in unnatural sexual relations. The *Tosafot* ultimately concluded that a husband can indeed engage in these practices, with certain conditions: "It is not considered like the act of Er and Onan unless it is his intention to destroy the seed, and it is his habit to always do so. However, if it is occasional, and the desire of his heart is to come upon his wife in an unnatural way, it is permitted." (*Tosafot* on Tractate *Yevamot* 34b) In other words, oral sex, anal sex, and mutual masturbation are permitted only if it is practiced occasionally and not as a couple's exclusive mode of sexual relations. The Rabbis of the Talmud agreed, stating, "During the twenty-four months, one may thresh within and winnow without." (Tractate *Yevamot* 34b) The context of this statement is that during the two years a woman was expected to breast feed her new baby, her husband was allowed to "thresh within"—that is, engage in vaginal intercourse—but "winnow without"—that is, ejaculate outside the vagina. This ruling was based on the idea that should a breast-feeding mother become pregnant while nursing, the new baby would deprive the older sibling of their mother's breast milk, which could dry up. The alternative was the mother could lose interest in breast-feeding her older infant. Therefore, to safeguard the health of the new baby, the Rabbis permitted the exact opposite of what Rambam ruled—namely, that a man can in fact engage in sexual behavior which will not result in pregnancy. The Rabbis assumed such non-coital sexual practices were acceptable provided that both the husband and the wife agreed and the purpose was mutual sexual pleasure.

As we have already seen, sex in the marital context should be mutually agreed upon and pleasurable for both partners. But not only was a man forbidden to force his wife to have sex, the Rabbis also forbade the withholding of sex as a form of punishment or blackmail against one's spouse. The Talmud states,

> If a woman rebels against her husband, [she can be penalized in that] her *ketubah* may be reduced by seven *dinars* [unit of coin] each week. . . . How long can this reduction continue? Until [she forfeits] the entire sum of her *ketubah*. And similarly, a man who rebels against his wife, the *ketubah* can be added on to by three *dinars* each week. (Mishnah *Ketubot* 5:7)

In a Jewish wedding, the *ketubah* was originally established to provide a measure of financial security for women, in case they were divorced or outlived their husbands. In the case of divorce or death, the *ketubah* stipulated that the ex-husband, or his heirs, had to pay the ex-wife, or widow, a certain amount of money until she could remarry, or provide herself with an independent source of income if she remained single. Therefore, if a woman were to refuse her husband sexually, having to survive on a reduced *ketubah* was a severe penalty. Similarly, a husband who refused his wife sexually had to raise the amount of the *ketubah* for each week he refused. The point of this passage, however, is to emphasize that sexual relations should not be hostage to the whims of husband or wife, but should be treated as a holy practice that draws a couple closer together.

In addition to partnership and pleasure, procreation is indeed a significant purpose of marital sex. After all, the very first commandment that God gave to human beings was to "be fertile and increase, fill the earth and master it." (Genesis 1:28) The prophet Isaiah echoed the sentiment that the world was created by God expressly to be populated by human beings. The prophet declared,

> For thus said the LORD,
> The Creator of heaven who alone is God,
> Who formed the earth and made it,
> Who alone established it—
> He did not create it a waste,
> But formed it for habitation:
> I am the LORD, and there is none else. [Isaiah 45:18]

The commandment to be "fertile and increase" is rather vague and led the Rabbis to discuss the extent of this mandate—that is, how many children must a couple have to fulfill this commandment? The houses of Shammai and Hillel, which disagreed about practically every matter of Jewish law, also disagreed about this topic: "A man should not abstain from being 'fertile and increasing' unless he already has two children. The House of Shammai says, 'two sons', but the House of Hillel says, 'a boy and a girl, as it says, "male and female He created them."'" (Genesis 5:2) (Mishnah *Yevamot* 6:6). Although each rabbinic school agreed that two children was the minimum number of children a couple must have in order to fulfill God's commandment, they disagreed over the gender of the children. The House of Shammai insisted a couple should have at least two boys, based on the example of Adam and Eve, who had two sons, Cain and Abel, and then subsequently had more children. However, the House of Hillel claimed a couple should have a boy and a girl, based on God's original act of creating humanity, by creating one male and one female. Despite the fact that these rabbinic schools argued about this topic, there is no officially sanctioned opinion within the Jewish tradition about the number or gender of children a Jewish couple is supposed to have to fulfill the commandment of "be fertile and increase." Because it is not within the power of every couple to have children, it seems inappropriate and insulting to apply standards that are not always within the realm of possibility.

Because of this, the Rabbis determined the maximum amount of time a couple should try to have children in order to fulfill this commandment. The passage above continues: "If he took a wife and lived with her ten years and she bore no child, he is not allowed to abstain [from the commandment of being fertile]. If he divorced her, she is permitted to be married to another man, and the second husband is then permitted to live with her for ten years." (Mishnah *Yevamot* 6:6) The Rabbis insisted that a man could not arbitrarily decide when to stop trying to have children. Although a husband was not required to divorce his wife in order to attempt to have children with another woman, it appears that this was a legitimate reason for divorce in rabbinic culture. Because the cause of the couple's infertility could in fact have been the husband's fault, the first wife was able to remarry. However, the ten-year time period began again for her new husband.

It is interesting that the Talmud sees the commandment to have children as devolving upon the man alone and not the woman. In fact, the Mishnah discusses this very subject: "It is the man who is commanded regarding 'be fertile and increase' and not the woman. But Rabbi Yochanon ben Broka taught, '[It is incumbent upon] both of them for it says, "And God blessed them and He said to them: Be fertile and increase."'" (Mishnah *Yevamot* 6:6) Rabbi Yochanon ben Broka challenged the anonymous view that only a man is commanded to have children and justified his opinion by quoting the Torah, emphasizing the fact that God spoke to both Adam and Eve when giving the command. In fact, the Hebrew commandment is couched in the plural. Regardless, Rabbi Broka's view was not accepted. However, later rabbis did determine that a woman shares equally in the commandment of procreation.

While the Torah commands all life to procreate and the Rabbis established parameters for fulfilling the mitzvah, procreation is ultimately beyond human control. However, these passages clearly indicate that even if a couple is unable to have children, they still are able to fulfill the first two purposes of marriage in the

Jewish tradition: namely, to provide mutual companionship and sexual pleasure for one another.

The one exception to the surprisingly open and liberal attitude of the Jewish tradition towards marital sexuality is that a couple is not permitted to have sexual relations during the wife's menstrual flow. Based on the Torah, the Rabbis developed a huge body of laws regarding what they called "family purity."

The Torah states, "Do not come near a woman when she is ritually impure with her menstrual flow to uncover her nakedness." (Leviticus 18:19) And it also says, "If a man lies with a woman in her infirmity and uncovers her nakedness—he has laid bare her flow and she has exposed her blood flow, both of them shall be cut off from among their people." (Leviticus 20:18) While the terms "ritually pure" and "impure" have negative connotations for modern Jews these words and their attendant concepts are actually quite neutral in this regard, especially in regard to ancient attitudes about women and sexuality.

It should also be noted that the ritual states of "purity" and "impurity" have nothing whatsoever to do with hygenic cleanliness. Rather, the terms "pure" and "impure" were applied equally to men and women and did not refer to any underlying assessment of the value of women in society. These words simply described ritual states of both men and women.

In ancient times, contact with corpses rendered a person ritually impure. In addition, whenever a person experienced a flow of blood, or other liquids (apart from urine) from their genitals, this rendered them ritually impure. Modern biblical scholars surmise that when a man experienced a nocturnal emission, or when a woman menstruated, the ancients understood this as a "life leak"—that is, a loss of their vital essence. They believed that a man or woman's capability to create new life was temporarily depleted, thus removing them from the state of being completely alive and rendering them closer to a state of death. Therefore, to safeguard the vitality of the rest of the community, such people were temporarily excluded from society until their "life leak" concluded, and they could be "purified" again by immersing in a body of water from a natural source—such as a spring, a river, or a cistern of rainwater—called a *mikvah*. During the time of menstruation, a woman was called being in *niddah*—that is, separated.

The Rabbis of the Talmud devoted an entire tractate, entitled *Niddah*, to the discussion of the laws of menstruation. Tractate *Niddah* states that from the first moment a woman notices her menstrual flow, she is forbidden to have sex with her husband. The Rabbis knew that although every woman's metabolism was different, the standard length of any woman's menstrual flow would be five days, including the first day it was noticed. The Rabbis ruled that the husband should literally maintain a physical separation from his wife during these days of *niddah*. Short of moving out of the house, the husband was not permitted to touch his wife, or even sleep in the same bed, lest such casual contact arouse their sexual desire and they inadvertently transgress these laws of *niddah*.

To ensure that the menstrual cycle had been completed, and also to ensure that a non-menstrual flow did not confuse the matter, the Rabbis determined that a woman must count seven full "clean" days after the fifth day of her period. This was to ensure a complete separation between the time when a woman experienced her menstrual flow and the time she was permitted to resume sexual relations with her husband. The term "clean" has nothing whatsoever to do with the hygenic state of the woman. Rather, it refers to the lack of menstrual blood during these days. Upon the conclusion of these twelve days of abstinence—five days of menstrual flow plus seven days of waiting—the woman was supposed to immerse herself in the pool of natural waters, the *mikvah*, in the evening of the twelfth day. At that point, the woman was free to resume sexual relations with her husband, until her next menstrual cycle.

Similar laws of ritual purity and impurity also applied to men who had experienced a nocturnal emission, or another type of flow of bodily fluid from the penis. However, such laws fell into desuetude during medieval times. The laws of *niddah* however have remained alive and part of the Jewish tradition to this day. Although primarily practiced in traditional Jewish communities, the laws of family purity are gaining new adherents in liberal Jewish communities. Many reasons and rationalizations have been given for maintaining this practice.

Traditional Approach: Many people find significance in these laws and rituals simply because they are an important aspect of a traditional Jewish life. These laws have been observed by Jews for thousands of years. Often times, the commandments which are the hardest to observe are precisely those which give their observers the greatest spiritual rewards and reinforcement.

Feminist Approach: Many women in modern times have seized upon the laws of *niddah* as a way of imbuing their Jewish existence with greater, uniquely feminine significance. It is an experience reserved for women that helps to reconnect them with their own bodily cycles each month in a religiously significant environment.

Philosophical Approach: Holiness can only be achieved through separation and self-discipline. Practicing regular abstinence from marital sex not only heightens sexual awareness between the couple, but serves to emphasize that it is a holy activity as well.

Symbolic Approach: A woman's menstruation is a symbolic brush with death involving a loss of blood, the life force. It also indicates a child will not be born from that egg. By immersing in the *mikvah*, a woman immerses herself in life, for the water is literally called, *mayim chayim*, or the "waters of life." This immersion, a symbolic revisiting of the birth waters of the womb each month, signals that the potential to create a new life begins again.

In conclusion, the Jewish tradition enunciates three distinct purposes for marriage: to provide partnership, mutual sexual pleasure, and to ensure the possibility of procreation. Marriage is the relationship that most closely resembles the spiritual relationship between God and the people of Israel. Therefore, sexuality is promoted as a means to enhance and deepen the connection between men and women, and ultimately, as a means to create holiness by making God's presence more tangible in our everyday lives.

Conclusion

The Jewish tradition is not monolithic, or even consistent. Beginning with the Torah, generations of scribes, rabbis, and scholars have struggled to interpret and articulate what they believed to be God's will. While the Jewish tradition claims that the Torah was revealed at Mt. Sinai, it also asserts that every generation of Jews has the obligation to reinterpret and explain the Torah so that it can be applied and enjoyed by all generations. Due to the rich diversity of human intellect and personal opinions, the Jewish tradition encompasses over 3,000 years of distinct and different individual convictions and explanations.

Does the Jewish tradition condone the use of deadly force for self-defense, or the use of marijuana, or pre-marital sex? It depends upon who you ask and what book you read. If there were a single, consistent and authoritative Jewish tradition, it would be possible to give clear and definitive answers to such vexing questions, but this is not the way of the Jewish tradition. On the contrary, the Jewish tradition values the questions more than the answers.

The purpose of this book is to raise questions. It is to provide readers with the resources to ask themselves challenging questions, and the material with which to ponder formidable areas of human life, such as how to control and channel feelings of anger, how to deal with alcohol and psychotropic substances, and how to act appropriately in fulfilling our sexual desires.

As creatures endowed by our Creator with free will, we have the responsibility and the freedom to choose for ourselves what we believe and how we behave. We must also be prepared to live with the consequences of our choices. The more informed we are, however, the wiser the choices we make. The Jewish tradition is an expansive, living treasure trove of insights and understanding. By contemplating its contents, decoding the classic texts, and engaging in debate with the Rabbis of old—as well as with modern rabbis—we can all learn to live better, more fulfilling lives. And even more importantly, how to lead lives imbued with holiness and the presence of the divine made manifest through all of our choices in life.

Glossary

Ad d'lo yada—Literally, "until he does not know." Name for the custom during the Jewish festival of Purim in which a person is encouraged to drink so much alcohol that they are no longer able to distinguish between the phrases "Blessed be Mordecai" and "Cursed be Haman."

Amidah—Literally, "standing." Refers to central Jewish prayer in all worship services.

Bar Mitzvah—Literally, "a son of the commandments." For a girl, "Bat Mitzvah," which means "a daughter of the commandments." This term is applied to boys at thirteen years old, and girls at twelve years old, when they are recognized as adult Jews, and thereby become subject to observing all of the commandments.

Beit ha-Mikdash—Literally, "House of the Sanctuary." The name of the first and second Temples which stood in Jerusalem and were centers of Jewish animal sacrificial worship. The first Temple was destroyed in 586 B.C.E. by the Babylonians, and the second Temple was destroyed by the Romans in 70 C.E.

Coitus interruptus—Latin for "interrupted sex." This refers to the practice of a man withdrawing his penis from a woman's vagina immediately before ejaculation to prevent pregnancy.

Dinars—A silver or gold coin. Derived from the Latin *denarius*.

Gehenna—Derived from the name "Gehinom," or "the valley of Hinom." An actual valley purportedly used by the Canaanites for child sacrifice. This name was applied by the Rabbis of the Talmud to a spiritual realm of suffering in the afterlife where wicked souls are punished. After completing the prescribed period of penance, all souls are admitted to the World to Come.

Gemara—Aramaic term meaning "learning." Refers to the rabbinic commentary, exposition, and analysis of the Mishnah by the Rabbis who lived in Israel and Babylonia from 220 C.E. to 500 C.E. Used as a synonym for the Talmud.

Gematria—Derived from the Greek word from which we get "geometry." This is the rabbinic practice of adding together the numerical equivalents of Hebrew letters in order to derive deeper meanings.

Get—The divorce document that a Jewish husband is required to give his wife in order to dissolve their marital relationship.

Gilui arayot—Literally, "exposing nakedness." Refers to immoral and abhorrent sexual contacts, such as rape, incest, or adultery.

Hekesh—Literally, "juxtaposition." A Talmudic principle of deriving meaning from two biblical verses or ideas that are close to one another in the text. The Rabbis determined that whatever applied to one situation also applied to the other.

Hofetz Hayyim—Literally, "He who wants life." The pen name for Rabbi Yisrael Meir Kagen (died 1933), a Polish rabbi who wrote many books about refraining from gossip and spreading rumors.

Iggeret HaKodesh—Literally, "the holy letter." Attributed to Rabbi Moses ben Nachman (Nachmonides) and written to his brother on the occasion of his marriage. This tract contains the intimate details of how a husband should make love to his wife.

Ish—"Man" in Hebrew. The word for woman, *ishah*, is derived from *Ish* and literally means, "from man," referring to the biblical story of the creation of Eve from Adam's rib.

Kaddish—Derived from the word for "holy." This is the name of a prayer recited by mourners in memory of a deceased family member.

Kadesh—Derived from the word for "holy," this refers to a cultic male prostitute found on the temple grounds of ancient Canaanite fertility sanctuaries. A female cultic prostitute was called a *kadesha*.

Kadosh—Literally, "holy." Biblical scholars surmise that an additional meaning might be "separate" or "apart."

kiddush—Derived from the word for "holy." This is the sanctification of the wine, a Hebrew prayer recited on *Shabbat* and Jewish holidays over a glass of wine to symbolize joy and gladness.

Kiddushin—Derived from the word for "holy." This refers to the betrothal ceremony in Jewish weddings whereby a man and woman become engaged.

Ketubah—This Jewish wedding contract stipulates that a husband promises to provide his wife with food, clothing, and regular sex. It also guarantees the woman a certain sum of money if she is divorced or widowed.

Lashon HaRah—Literally, "evil tongue." Malicious, or derogatory comments about other people that are prohibited in the Jewish tradition, but are actually true. If they are false, they would be *motzi shem rah*, literally, "bringing forth a bad name."

Log—An ancient measure of liquid volume equivalent to the contents of approximately six large eggs.

Mamzer (plural: *mamzerim*)—Literally, "bastard." The child of an adulterous sexual union. Such children are subject to lifelong discrimination in the Jewish tradition, which is also passed down to their children.

Mayim chayim—Literally, "living waters" or "the waters of life." This refers to the kind of water used to fill a *mikvah*, a Jewish ritual bath. Such water can only come from a pure, natural source, such as a rainfall, a spring, a river, snow melt, or the ocean.

Midrash—Literally, "exposition" or "explanation." This refers to the folktales and lore created by the Rabbis to fill in gaps in the biblical narratives and to inject their own values and creative ideas into the fabric of the Jewish tradition.

Mishnah—The first codification of rabbinic law, created, organized, and recorded following the destruction of the second Temple in 70 C.E. and finalized in 220 C.E.

Mishneh Torah—Literally, "second Torah." A multi-volume codification of Jewish law composed by Rabbi Moses ben Maimon (Maimonides) in 1177. Considered an ancient but authoritative work of Jewish law to this day.

Mikvah—The ritual bath for spiritual purification of both men and women in the Jewish tradition. The waters must come from a pure, natural source such as a rainfall, a spring, a river, snow melt, or the ocean.

Mitzvah—Literally, "commandment." Refers to all activities that are understood as God's commandments, enumerated in the Torah and further expanded by the Rabbis in the Talmud.

Motzi shem rah—Literally, "bringing forth a bad name." Malicious, derogatory gossip about other people which is prohibited in the Jewish tradition. Such information is by definition false. If it is true, it is *Lashon Ha-Rah* or "evil tongue."

Nazarite—Derived from the Hebrew word meaning "vow." A nazarite was someone, a man or woman, who would temporarily and voluntarily take on ascetic practices. A nazarite could be any person who swore to temporarily abstain from cutting their hair, coming into contact with the dead, and drinking wine. People would become nazarites in order to achieve a high degree of holiness and sanctity, either in gratitude for surviving some event or to fulfill a promise made in a time of hardship.

Niddah—Literally, "separate." Refers to a woman during her menstrual period and the rabbinic requirements that the husband and wife temporarily abstain from sexual relations during her menstruation. Also the name of a tractate in the Talmud devoted to this topic.

Onah—Literally, "her appointed time." Refers to the regular sexual relations that a Jewish husband is required to provide his wife.

Passover—One of the three major pilgrimage holidays in the Jewish calendar that celebrates the Exodus of the Israelites from Egypt. It is characterized by the celebration of the seder.

Pilegesh—Literally, "concubine." In the Hebrew Bible and rabbinic literature, a legitimate and accepted member of some households in ancient society who functioned as a wife but was not afforded the same status.

Purim—Literally, "lots." A minor Jewish festival that celebrates the downfall of Haman, an antisemitic royal

Persian advisor, at the hands of the Jewish queen, Esther, and her uncle, Mordecai.

Rabbis—Refers to the first generations of Jewish spiritual leaders who lived and functioned from 70 C.E. till 500 C.E. These Rabbis were the first ones to interpret and update the Torah so that it would make sense to the Jews of their generation. They produced the Mishnah, the Talmud, and Midrash.

Rechilut—Literally, a "tale bearer." Refers to derogatory information which is either true or false, positive or negative, but always unsubstantiated.

Rodef—Literally, "pursuer." In rabbinic law, it was permitted to use deadly force without forewarning against a *rodef*, someone who was pursuing after another person in order to prevent them from committing potential murder or rape.

Sanhedrin—The grand rabbinic court of justice which used to adjudicate civil and criminal cases in ancient times. Also the name of a Talmud tractate that describes the function of this court.

Satan—Literally, "adversary." This was the title and role description of the angel assigned to argue against the merits of the people of Israel in God's heavenly court of justice.

Seder—Literally, "order." The evening festive meal devoted to the recounting and celebration of the Exodus from Egypt. One of the hallmarks of the seder is drinking four cups of wine spaced throughout the retelling.

Sefer HaEshkol—Literally, "the book of grape clusters." Written by Rabbi Abraham ben Isaac of Narbonne, France, this was the first Jewish legal code compiled in southern France, and later served as a model for subsequent codifications. Due to its influence, it was quoted frequently by Rabbi Yosef Karo in the *Shulchan Aruch.*

Shabbat—Literally, "rest." Refers to Saturday, the seventh day of the week, the traditional day of rest and sanctification for the Jewish people. Considered the holiest day of the year, it is characterized by communal prayer, family meals, and the cessation of work activities.

Shulchan Aruch—Literally, a "set table." The classic medieval code of law written by Rabbi Yosef Karo in northern Israel and published in 1567. A comprehensive and authoritative work of Jewish law to this day.

Talmud—Literally, "learning." Refers to the Mishnah and the Gemara as a combined work. This is the classic text of rabbinic exposition and interpretation of the Torah. Written in Aramaic by the Rabbis who lived from 70 C.E. to 500 C.E.

Tosafot—Literally, "Additions." A medieval commentary on the Talmud and the commentary of Rashi. Written by a number of rabbis spanning several generations who lived in France in the 13th century.

Tractate—A volume of the Talmud or Mishnah.

Yetzer ha-rah—Literally, the "evil inclination." This refers to such basic human instincts as envy, material desires, greed, and lust. The *yetzer ha-rah* is a necessary and crucial component of human life for without it, the Rabbis claim that no man would ever establish a home, marry and raise children or engage in business.

Yetzer ha-tov—Literally, the "good inclination." This refers to such basic human instincts as selflessness, compassion, pity, and altruism. The *yetzer ha-tov* is the balancing force which helps to maintain an equilibrium with the *yetzer ha-rah*, the "evil inclination."

Yod—The tenth letter of the Hebrew alphabet.

Z'nut—Literally, "promiscuity." Degraded sex which serves no purpose other than immediate physical gratification. This type of sexual contact is prohibited in the Jewish tradition.

Zonah—Literally, "prostitute." It was forbidden for Jewish men and women to be prostitutes, or to visit them. They were associated with ancient Canaanite sexual fertility practices and thus, were considered an abomination.

Index

About the Author

Rabbi Daniel Kohn is a natural educator. He has received degrees from Washington University in St. Louis and the University of Judaism, and was ordained from the Jewish Theological Seminary of America. Rabbi Kohn has created and taught relevant, challenging Jewish curricula to teenagers and adults in formal and informal settings, Jewish camps, Hillels, synagogue schools, and day schools both in the United States and Israel. As a founding faculty member of the Solomon Shechter High School of Long Island, Rabbi Kohn published numerous articles about Jewish education in the *Jewish Spectator, Journal of Jewish Education, Conservative Judaism, United Synagogue Review*, and *Gleanings* (the Melton Journal), as well as authored, *Practical Pedagogy for the Jewish Classroom: Classroom Management, Instruction, and Curriculum Development* (Greenwood Publishing Group, Educators' Reference Collection, 1999). A second degree black belt in Aikido, Rabbi Kohn also volunteers for the Ask-a-Rabbi service on America Online (www.jewish.com). He resides in California with his wife, Deborah Stachel, and daughter, Nava.